# YOUR INCOME, YOUR LIFE

How Modern Day Families Can Live Happy,
Healthy, and Wealthy on Any Income.

**Jeff Bouwman**

Published by Motivational Press, Inc.
1777 Aurora Road
Melbourne, Florida, 32935
www.MotivationalPress.com

Copyright 2017 © by Jeff Bouwman
All Rights Reserved

No part of this book may be reproduced or transmitted in any form by any means: graphic, electronic, or mechanical, including photocopying, recording, taping or by any information storage or retrieval system without permission, in writing, from the authors, except for the inclusion of brief quotations in a review, article, book, or academic paper. The authors and publisher of this book and the associated materials have used their best efforts in preparing this material. The authors and publisher make no representations or warranties with respect to accuracy, applicability, fitness or completeness of the contents of this material. They disclaim any warranties expressed or implied, merchantability, or fitness for any particular purpose. The authors and publisher shall in no event be held liable for any loss or other damages, including but not limited to special, incidental, consequential, or other damages. If you have any questions or concerns, the advice of a competent professional should be sought.

Manufactured in the United States of America.

ISBN: 978-1-62865-368-7

# CONTENTS

DEDICATION . . . . . . . . . . . . . . . . . . . . . . . . . . . . . . . . . . . 5
ACKNOWLEDGEMENTS . . . . . . . . . . . . . . . . . . . . . . . . . . . 6
FOREWORD . . . . . . . . . . . . . . . . . . . . . . . . . . . . . . . . . . . 8
INTRODUCTION . . . . . . . . . . . . . . . . . . . . . . . . . . . . . . . 10
MY STORY AND THIS BOOK . . . . . . . . . . . . . . . . . . . . . . . 15

CHAPTER 1
  YOU ARE NOT ALONE. . . . . . . . . . . . . . . . . . . . . . . . . . . 31
CHAPTER 2
  MONEY IS AN ACQUIRED TASTE . . . . . . . . . . . . . . . . . . . 39
CHAPTER 3
  UNDERSTANDING THE IMPACT OF DEBT ON OUR LIVES . . . . 49
CHAPTER 4
  THAT MONEY FEELING . . . . . . . . . . . . . . . . . . . . . . . . . 58
CHAPTER 5
  YOUR TRUE COST OF LIVING . . . . . . . . . . . . . . . . . . . . . 63
CHAPTER 6
  LIVING LIFE ON YOUR OWN TERMS . . . . . . . . . . . . . . . . . 68
CHAPTER 7
  TIME IS MORE IMPORTANT THAN THINGS . . . . . . . . . . . . . 75
CHAPTER 8
  BUDGETING FOR A PARENT'S LIFE . . . . . . . . . . . . . . . . . 81
CHAPTER 9
  THE THREE LEVELS OF FAMILY FINANCE. . . . . . . . . . . . . . 94

CHAPTER 10
**HOW MUCH DEBT IS TOO MUCH?** .................... 101

CHAPTER 11
**BUDGETING FOR STABILITY**.......................... 112

CHAPTER 12
**THE IMPROVEMENT PATH** ........................... 123

CHAPTER 13
**GROWTH AND ACCUMULATION** ..................... 140

CHAPTER 14
**TEACH IN THE MOMENT** ............................ 147

CHAPTER 15
**BALANCING WORK, LIFE, & FAMILY** .................. 152

**WRAP UP**........................................ 159

# DEDICATION

I dedicate this book to you. For having the courage to explore your relationship with money, and for wanting to create something different for your future.

I dedicate this book to my wife. For inspiring me to be a better person, for helping me see what is important in life, and for listening to me ramble on about this book. You are the love of my life and I am grateful to spend my moments with you each and every day!

I dedicate this book to my three amazing daughters. Avery, Irelyn, and Harper. You have made me a better person in ways you may never know. I am learning from you every day and hope that I can model something more, so that you will be inspired to be more.

Finally, I dedicate this book to my parents. For allowing me to learn from my own mistakes and teaching me that money, in fact, does not grow on trees.

# ACKNOWLEDGEMENTS

**Jim Sheils:** Author of the Family Board Meeting

I am inspired by your mission to deepen relationships and improve education for families. Thank you for creating the education matrix and challenging the status quo, and thank you for being a part of this book!

**Jason Mackenzie:** Author of *The Dadly Book of Open*

Thank you for encouraging me to share my story, and giving me the permission I needed to help others in a more purposeful way. Without you, this book would not be a reality.

**Gene Villeneuve:** Author at *BusinessHealthResults.com*

I inspire to create the life you have and wish the best for you and your family.

Thank you for sharing your financial lessons with me, and now with the world.

**Neil McKay:** Author at *PerpetualKinetics.com*

Your friendship means the world to me and I couldn't have done this without your help.

Thank you for the time and effort you put into providing the first feedback and edits on the book.

**Larry Hagner**: Author of *The Dads Edge*

Thank you for creating a wonderful community where humble fathers can come together and grow as individuals, and as parents.

**Armando Cruz and Lance Salazar**

You are both an inspiration to me and I am grateful to have you in my life. Thank you for sharing your words of wisdom and providing insights on my final draft of the book.

# FOREWORD

With the exception of personal development, I have found no subject more needed in our schools than that of financial intelligence. We see this lack of education carry over into adulthood and money issues can consume our focus and hinder some of our most meaningful relationships.

But does it need to be like this? Can this pattern of financial struggle be extinguished?

Working with scores of families over the years, I can honestly say it does not need to be like this. The patterns of financial struggle can be broken.

The starting point is to gain a base of knowledge and a simple plan of action. The pages within this book provide just that, a firm strategy and a place to start. What I loved most about Jeff's approach to this book is his vulnerability. He shares struggles, breaking points, and a road to recovery and abundance that anyone can follow.

With a simple working knowledge and doable plan to gain financial strength, your finances can dramatically improve in a short amount of time. Your stress levels can drastically decrease. Your relationships can be given the proper time and attention you've always desired to give them.

Unfortunately, personal finance is still a taboo subject. For some, financial intelligence is still frowned upon because financial intelligence is equal to promoting greed.

I have found the opposite.

# FOREWORD

The best education around financial intelligence teaches that money is not what it is all about. Money is not the most important thing. We can control its use and its effect. We can enjoy our most treasured relationships and money issues do not need to over shadow them.

Society has made most people ashamed or depressed to admit their struggles with finance, but that is where the magic really begins. It's your first big step to say to hell with the Jones's. Keep in mind, the Jones's are usually broke, in debt, and emotionally bankrupt. The nice stuff around them does little to offset the pains of reality.

Take the road less travelled. Make that which is your priority, the priority. The pages ahead will open new doors, re-write negative paradigms and supply you with rhythms that can re-ground your financial life on your terms.

To your greatest wealth and abundance,

Jim Sheils

Author

The Family Board Meeting

# INTRODUCTION

When I started on my journey to find financial health, I read every book I could find. I listened to podcasts, and scoured the internet for information. The more I read the more confused I felt. I already knew what these books were telling me, and was tired of hearing about all of the things I had done wrong. As a parent I felt alone, and I felt frustrated.

I wasn't in a financial crisis, but I had an overwhelming feeling of guilt and anxiety when it came to our finances. It seemed like every time I had a difficult challenge in my life, my finances suffered as a result. I was still living paycheck to paycheck, and had more debt than I wanted. Worst of all, these feelings were having an impact on my interactions with my kids. It was affecting how they saw me today, and I knew it was going to affect how they saw me later in life.

I felt like the experts were writing to someone else. I remember thinking that I just wanted to live the life I deserved, and give my kids the same. I was desperately looking for a way to manage our debt and improve our cash flow, without living a life of sacrifice. I didn't feel I should have to sacrifice, if I really didn't need to. I didn't want to ask my kids to forego the things I did when I was growing up.

I felt like it was my income, and my life, and I wanted to live it on my own damn terms.

If you are anything like I was a couple of years ago, you look back over what you make each year, and wonder where it all went. How is it that no matter how much you make, your finances still seem to hold you back?

When you are at work, you are thinking about being at home, and when you are at home, you are thinking about work. Each week it seems like there is a new expense you didn't see coming. You spend less and less on yourself, but fund your life like you always did in the past. You borrow from tomorrow, to fund what is best for your family today.

As you weave your way through your parenting journey, one question keeps playing in your head: "How can we give our kids what they need, while taking enough time away from work to be with them?" The balancing act between work, home, kids, and your finances, is causing your stress levels to increase. Perhaps, like me, your patience is wearing thin, and you don't feel you are being the person you want to be. Both at home, and at work.

Maybe you are struggling to control your finances and looking to create stability for you and your family? Maybe you are trying to find a way to instil discipline with your money and manage your debt? Maybe you already have your situation in control, but you are trying to find ways to take your finances to the next level, for yourself, and for your family.

Either way, I can tell you I understand what you are feeling. I am just like you. In fact, I am you. No matter what your current relationship is with money, I can relate. I struggled to balance my work and my life. I struggled to make a dent in our mountain of debt, despite making a good living, and having a background in money. My financial struggles were holding me back from developing as a husband, and as a father, and my relationships suffered as a result.

## INTRODUCTION

When I had a problem with money I would have never admitted it to anyone. I didn't even admit it to myself. But now that I have come to terms with my problems and created a new path, I want to share my story with you. I want others to know what I discovered.

Most parents have strong feelings and emotions when it comes to their money. They are looking for ways to be better with their family finances. What most parents are realizing is the only person who can control the decisions we make with our money is ourselves. What works for one parent may or may not work for another, and you need to figure out what is best for your circumstance. When you actively seek out information and educate yourself, you will find that you can start making choices based on the life you want to live, instead of the life of others.

Yes, there are many great books out there on specific personal financial strategies. I have read most of them. What I have done in this book is package those thoughts in a manner which gives you the power to understand your relationship with money, and make choices for how you want that relationship to be in the future. The methods I talk about are simple and straightforward to use, and can help you define how you want money to affect your kids. They will set your kids up to better handle the challenges they will inevitably face over the course of their life.

I am not hiding my problems anymore. If sharing my story can help someone else avoid the mistakes I made, then it is worth it. If sharing my story can help free up the anxiety people today have with money, it will be worth it. If sharing my story can help others improve their debt management discipline, it will be worth it. If sharing my story helps others create a better financial value system for their kids, it will be worth it!

## INTRODUCTION

I want you to appreciate your time, more than you appreciate your things. My hope is that you want more from your relationships, than you do money. I want you to see that your finances are not just yours; they are also your family's. It is time to put the "we," back in wealth.

The financial concepts in this book are not new. There is nothing in here that will revolutionize the way we manage money, and I offer no magic pills for becoming rich. I simply recognize it is your money, and it is up to you as to how you manage it. It is your income, and it is your life. I want you to live it on your terms.

I am a father and a husband, and I have made many mistakes along my financial journey. That is only part of what makes me qualified to write this book. I am also an accountant and have worked for years in both personal and corporate finance. I have seen both sides of personal finance, and I know that the industry is constantly evolving. I want us to evolve with it. I know that you will not change unless you choose to make that change. I only hope this book helps you get some of the financial education that we didn't receive when we were kids, and if a change is required, you are open to admitting it.

Parents in the modern era are educating themselves more than any other generation in the past. They want more for their kids. Not because they are struggling, but because they want better. This book is packaged in a way that will provide you with a pathway to better.

If you read this book and make the decision to change your relationship with money by applying the steps I outline, I guarantee you will free yourself from the money myths that have been holding you back. You will finally have more time to spend with your family, significantly improve your relationship with your partner, find financial health, and enhance your personal and parenting wealth.

Don't be the person who misses out on opportunities in life because you have bought into what society is selling. Don't let your relationship with money hold you back. Be the kind of family other people look at and question. Be the kind of family other people see and say, "I don't know how they do it."

It's your life, and your income. Make the decision to take back control of your finances right now, and enjoy the new life you're creating for yourself, and your family. I have found that when we embark on a journey of self-discovery, what we often find is that the journey itself is the discovery!

# MY STORY AND THIS BOOK

I graduated from the University of Waterloo with a Bachelor of Arts, specializing in Accountancy. I went on to complete my designation, and took several additional finance courses. In 1999, I completed the Canadian Securities course, and got a job at one of the most known financial services firms in North America. From the outside looking in, I was a financial success. I looked the part, and I played the part.

- My co-workers wore nice clothes and drove fancy cars; so did I.
- They went to expensive restaurants for lunches and ordered expensive bottles of wine; so did I.
- They had courtside tickets for the Raptors games and bought platinum level Leafs tickets. I went too.
- Our brokers would get concert tickets from mutual fund companies, and I would go too.
- Many brokers went for drinks in the bar in our building after work each day, and I went too.

I played the part very well. I was by modern-day terms, successful. But the truth was, I was broke. I struggled to get by, living paycheck to paycheck.

As the accountant on staff, I would reconcile payroll every other week and look at the lofty salaries the people made in our company. I would dream about making that too. I thought about all the things I could buy and do, if I was making that kind of money. But behind closed doors I was broke, and I never let anyone I worked with, or my parents, know it. In their minds, for all I could tell, they saw me as successful.

Four years passed, and the company I worked with was sold to a big bank. As the senior financial leader, I was retained on a bonus to ensure that I didn't leave while the acquisition was happening. Finally, I was making the big bucks all of my co-workers had been earning for years!

Before the doors closed, I was offered a job with the bank, but it meant I would have to give up my three-month severance package. I would have to keep making the money I had before, and I would still be in Toronto living paycheck to paycheck. I opted for the severance package. I knew that I could get a job quickly because I had great experience and my background was in something every company needed: accounting. For the first time in my life, I was going to have some money saved up. I opened up a retirement savings account and deposited my severance check into it.

My last day of work was at the beginning of July in 2003, and the very next day, I landed a job offer from a company in London, Ontario. Better yet, the job didn't start until September. I viewed this as a huge success.

I did what most 27-year-old men would do, I rewarded myself and purchased a brand new Infiniti QX4. I financed it because I knew I could afford the $700 a month payment, living in a city like London with a significantly lower cost of living. Heck, I deserved a reward like this for all of my hard work.

I was now living in London and things were going well. I was in a committed relationship, we had two brand new cars, and we had just purchased our first house. We took advantage of the first time homebuyer's plan and withdrew everything from that investment account I had just opened up. People couldn't see the investment account, so I figured it could wait. What they could see were the brand new cars parked in the driveway of our brand new home.

From the outside looking in, I was successful.

Money wasn't something we talked about in our relationship because we both worked and it wasn't an issue. In fact, we struggled with pretty much everything else in our lives so money didn't have time to come up. We continued to buy things for the house because we were trying to find things to make us happy. We needed our house to look perfect, because our relationship was far from it.

When that relationship ended, we got very lucky with our money. We were able to sell the house and take enough from the equity to start over again. When I look back, I can remember sitting down and working through our money situation for the first time in our relationship. How ironic that our first money conversation would happen, when our relationship had come to an end. The conversation went well, and for the first time in several months I actually felt like we were communicating. I didn't realize it until recently, but money actually helped us communicate, and it was one of the things we had had in common all along.

It wasn't my decision to end the relationship, so I struggled for a long time after. I was beaten down trying to figure out what had gone wrong, and I spent days and months grieving the loss. As I looked for any form of gratification, many days I found it by buying things I really didn't need. Was that the best way for me to deal with my emotions? Probably not. But it is what I needed to do at the time in order to get by.

I eventually went on to purchase a smaller house and furnished it with everything a new bachelor would need. I replaced my brand new 32-inch TV, with a new 53-inch TV. I put it up on a wall that could barely hold it. I had a hot tub in the backyard, a new elliptical to whip myself into shape, new leather furniture for entertaining, and a custom made poker table for the basement. It was one of the nicest bachelor pads I could buy. But I still wasn't happy.

I would sit in darkness at night for hours on end struggling to come to terms with a failed relationship. I was almost 30 years old and I didn't have any solid relationships to show for it. My friends from university were gone because I alienated them when I was working so much to pay off my debts. My unhealthy relationship with money had pushed away the people that could have helped me the most.

Eventually, after asking for help, and with a lot of love and support, I managed to get through and come out stronger. I figured out that I had to invest in myself and find ways to make myself happy, if I ever wanted to make anyone else happy. I built up a network of friends once again, and started doing more of the hobbies I had let go when I was younger. From the outside looking in, I once again looked successful.

My path to self-discovery helped me find some happiness and fulfillment, but most of it was still associated with spending. In the process of redefining my relationship with myself, I still hadn't looked at my relationship with money.

Have you ever purchased something only to later regret it?

Better yet, have you ever purchased something, come up with a lie to justify why it made sense, and secretly regretted that purchase each and every day? I have.

During these single years of my life I would routinely go out and buy designer clothes at ridiculous prices, because I had convinced myself I looked better in them. I convinced myself I felt better in them, and they would last much longer than any other clothes money could buy. I once spent over $1500 on three shirts, and $700 on a pair of jeans. Did I look better? Let's just say that I could have paid for a lot of private personal training sessions for that $2200 and looked a hell of a lot better in clothes from Walmart.

Have you ever gone out for dinner and drinks, multiple nights in a week, and forgotten how much you spent? I have. I used to buy dinner out at least three times a week, and convinced myself it was cheaper than cooking for one. I usually had three or more drinks with each of those meals, and spent the time socializing with friends because going out made me happy. I know now that we could have socialized in the comfort of our own homes and ate healthier and cheaper than at any restaurant.

Have you ever had more than 75% of your annual income tied up in the cars in your driveway? I have. I lived alone, and still owned two brand new vehicles. The sports car was in the garage polished and ready to impress, while the truck sat in the driveway so that I could get to work safely during the winter. To make it worse, I actually traded in my first brand new sports car only six months after purchasing it, because I convinced myself that the dealership was treating me poorly. I convinced myself that the $15,000 loss I had just taken was justified because of poor customer service. Ouch.

I went on to purchase another sports car, this time a very expensive one. I convinced myself that I shouldn't have to wait until I was fifty or for my mid-life crisis to own the car of my dreams. It was a Corvette, and not just any Corvette: it was a Z06. It sat in the garage almost every day of the week because I wanted to keep it looking as impressive as possible. Over the course of eighteen months, I only put five thousand kilometers on it, and eventually sold it as well (at yet another huge loss).

Have you ever gone months on end without creating a budget or looking at your personal finances? I have. At one point in time, I went three months without even logging on to my banking account. In the previous era where we used printed bank books, that is like going three months without visiting your bank all together. You spend and spend, without any regard for what is happening behind the scenes. When I finally did log in, I was shocked to see that I was actively taking advantage of my over-draft protection that I had purchased years before. It had become my own form of a personal line of credit, and it was at a ridiculously high interest rate.

My spending was a good representation to the outside world of my success in life. I was successful. Each time I made more money, I spent more money. Each time I would spend more money, I would have to make more money. I would go on to work longer hours, and take on more responsibility in my career, because I had to. Sure, I convinced myself that I was successful; that climbing the corporate ladder was as clear sign of dedication and achievement. In reality, it was a vicious battle of income vs life.

## THE TIDE STARTED SHIFTING

In 2008, I finally started to see there might be something more to life than a career. I started to see that money might not be the source of happiness, and perhaps true contentment would be found with love.

For the first time in my life, I saw first-hand the love a parent can have for a child, and I saw it at the worst of times. It was when my sister lost her second child, who was only three years old at the time.

I spent hours and days with my sister trying to comfort her through that difficult time. I hugged her when she needed to cry and tried to find words to help her. I tried to be strong for her so that she could figure out how to move on. For the first few days, I didn't cry at all, because I was the shoulder that was to be cried on.

I stayed with her for the week that followed.

I will never forget walking outside the funeral home after seeing my nephew for the first time after his death. Inside, I was strong for my sister, but when I walked outside by myself, I shriveled up into a heaping mess. I cried uncontrollably. I not only felt the pain of losing a nephew, I could feel the pain that my sister had as well. After 20 minutes, I wiped away the tears, put on my strong face, and went back inside to support my sister.

When I finally made the drive back to London, I did a lot of thinking. I kept the radio off and started to think about what I needed in my life. I knew in this moment that everything I had set-up in my life was completely backwards to what it should be. I was looking for happiness in the wrong places, and I needed to open up my heart to the possibility of finding love. That time of solitude in the car, was just what I needed. I knew I was done looking to advance my career; I was done trying to buy happiness, I was done trying to be something on the outside that I wasn't on the inside.

I often think back and reflect on watching the balloons rise up into the air at my nephew's funeral. That moment will never leave my mind. It is a constant reminder to live life at one hundred percent, and to enjoy the moments we have before us. It is that moment that I feel in my heart and in my stomach when I am struggling with things that I shouldn't in life. It was that moment that makes me want my kids to enjoy their youth, because I know they will never have the opportunity again.

I found love again shortly after, and it is the kind of love most men dream about. I feel closer to my wife as each day passes, and she makes me want to be better. In February 2011, we had our first child together, and I felt what I coveted so many years before; the love that a parent feels for their child. I am blessed to have felt that three times.

## SOMETIMES YOU HAVE TO TAKE A STEP BACK, TO MOVE FORWARD

Unfortunately, as a parent, my spending habits not only continued, they got worse. We wanted our kids to have more because that is what our parents wanted for us. We bought what we thought our kids needed, and provided them with the things that would make their lives better. We didn't cut expenses in other areas of our lives, we just spent more in this wonderful new area. Our relationship with money was unhealthy, and as it turns out, I hadn't learned anything from my failed relationship years before.

The more kids we had, the more we spent. The more we spent, the more I had to make. The more I had to make, the more I worked. The more I worked, the guiltier I felt about not being present for my family. I internalized all of it, and my blood pressure was getting worse with the passing of every year. Still, I never talked to my family about our finances, because I thought I was protecting them.

Our finances were in a bad state, and I knew I was one emergency away from a total financial, or mental, meltdown. I knew my personal and financial values were in conflict, but at the time I couldn't see why.

We had my in-laws over for dinner one Friday evening, and we were talking about real estate. I had considered buying a rental property to help us create some positive net worth, and I was interrupted mid-sentence.

I was saying *"When I make my next million, I am going to..."*

And my wife interrupted with:

*"What do you mean next million? What did you do with the first?"*

I was in shock, and felt an overwhelming sense of shame. In reality, I had spent over a million dollars before I had turned 30, and now almost ten years later, we had hardly any equity to show for it. In that moment, I realized what I should have realized so much earlier in my life. Money shouldn't be so taboo, and I shouldn't have kept my finances from the people closest to me. I had been taking on all the burden of the financial stress in our household, and the people that could have helped me the most were still the dark. They had no idea how unhealthy my relationship with money was. The burden was all on my shoulders, and I deserved every ounce of it.

## MY STORY AND THIS BOOK

This realization happened in 2014 and we were about to come to a major crossroad. I had spent the first three and a half years of my kids' lives waiting until the last possible minute in the morning to leave for work. This was in an effort to see everyone before I left for the day. Then, at the end of the day, my wife would wait as long as possible to start baths, so that I could have some time with the kids before bed. I struggled to get home each and every day. Some days I would be in the garage still on my phone and my family didn't even know I had arrived. If I didn't make it in by 7:30, I knew it would be too late. That happened too many times.

We had new leadership in our company and their approach with people wasn't in line with my values. Stress was building, and I knew I wasn't being the best father or husband I could be. I lived in guilt twenty-four hours a day. When I was at home I felt guilty about not being at work, and my mind would race with the things I needed to do at the office. When I was at home, I felt guilty about not being at work, and my heart would ache for the time when I could leave.

My girls were going to grow up whether I was present or not. They were growing up, and I wasn't present. But I wanted to be. No amount of money in the world was worth the stress that I was living with. No amount of money in the world was justification for not being present with my family even when I was physically there. I needed a change.

With the decisions our parent company had taken away from us at work, I knew the next year was going to be financially difficult. I knew I was going to make half of what I did the year before. I knew we had to make changes with our finances or something bad was going to happen.

Finally, I was ready to examine our finances, and the impact my behaviors were having on my life.

## WANTING DIFFERENT

I knew I wanted something different. I didn't want our kids to make the same mistakes I had made. I knew they watched and listened to everything we did, and I wanted them to have a different opportunity in life. It was time to re-define my relationship with money and improve the relationships in my life.

After updating the budget at work and our personal budget at home, I realized that I had only nine months to get our finances back in order. With the purchase of two new vehicles and having built a custom home, we had racked up an astonishing amount of debt in a very short period of time. Debt that we would not possibly be able to pay off, using my base salary alone.

The compensation structure I was on, consisted of fifty percent base salary and fifty percent bonus. Our bonuses were based on divisional profitability, and over the past three years, our division had done quite well. Looking ahead to 2015, I knew that was about to change and we would be forced to live off of my base salary alone. We had to change too if we wanted to get through this.

We eventually paid off 75 percent of that debt in those 9 months, and after the dust had settled, I knew there was a bigger issue to deal with.

Things I thought I controlled in the office, I no longer could. Things that would directly impact my pay. When I questioned those decisions, I was told by my boss to "suck it up."

Do I? Should I just change my beliefs about leadership and just carry on? Should I throw my values out the window and forget everything I had learned? Should I stop treating others the way I want to be treated? These VPs treated people like garbage each and every day, and I hated it.

The stress and anxiety from work had made me miserable at home. While I pretended at work, by the end of the day, I couldn't pretend at home. My need to make more money was destroying the life I had so desperately wanted. My income was driving my life, and it wasn't a life I would be able to look back upon and be proud of.

10 years earlier in my career I likely would have stayed and I would have changed. But not at this point in my life—too much was at stake. What example would I be setting for my kids?

I had accomplished what I committed to in my job. I had done that, despite of it all.

I knew that it was time to turn the page and start again. And I knew I needed to take some time with my family to be a better father to my daughters. I needed to be better to my wife.

## QUITTING IS NEVER EASY

While I knew I wouldn't find another job in the area that made the same money, I had done the math and knew I would be ok. With the team I had behind me at home, and our new financial landscape, we only had to make some small adjustments to our expenses and we could live off less. We would be OK.

I sat down with my boss and started a sequence of several tough conversations. We agreed quickly that I would leave my current position. I was then asked to fill a different role for another group. I agreed, and we set forth to negotiate what my new contract would look like. Unfortunately, it wasn't a fun negotiation, and in the process I realized that the only person that was going to look out for me was, in fact, me.

The next 4 months our negotiations continued, and the VPs pushed us to work longer and longer hours to fix issues they also played a role in creating. It was an extremely difficult time on my family and I never knew if the next day would be my last day. But I knew one of them could be. In fact many days I hoped the next would be my last because I was out of contract and I didn't need the additional stress. I was on edge and I couldn't show it at work because that would not make me the leader I wanted to be. I tried hard not to show it at home as well, but I struggled and my wife was left to pick up a lot of the pieces.

The entire process I had just gone through made me realize my definition of success was screwed up! I pushed our corporate office to put a new contract in front of me, and gave them a deadline to do so by. I sought legal counsel and knew the steps and told them I wouldn't be in the following week if we hadn't sorted it out.

I had realized they didn't care if I stayed or not, and I wouldn't be getting a contract that made sense. More importantly, I wouldn't be getting a contract that was worth taking, because my values were obviously different than theirs. Nevertheless, I stayed until 6pm right to the last day I worked there, and when I finally got the offer for the other position, I declined it.

Within days of leaving I found myself more present with my family. I was laughing and joking with them again. I wasn't sweating the small stuff. By seeing my actions through my children's eyes, I was finally able to see that I needed to better with finances, if I wanted to better in the other areas of my life. I now believe finances are one of the key elements on a continuum, in which we must focus on being better.

I believe we can live our lives at 100 percent, if and when we make healthy choices with our money. I believe we can all openly talk about finances, if we focus on aligning our values with our actions. I have come to realize that my personal finances are not defined by the income I am making, but instead by the life I choose to lead.

My hope is that through my experiences you will see your personal finances as a choice as well. If I can help you realize that being rich has more to do with the size of your life, than the size of your bank account, I will have succeeded.

## ABOUT THIS BOOK

In this book I reveal how many successful parents are building financial health and wealth in the modern era. The path to financial freedom is translating into a life based on abundance for many. It can for you to.

People often ask me how are we able to live off half of the income we did before. They ask me how we paid off so much debt in such a short period of time, while leaving the job I worked my entire career to get.

For the first time, I am going to answer these exact questions for you. I am going to explain how I freed up 30 hours a week so that I could spend it with my family, how talking about money improved my relationship with my spouse, and how aligning my financial and personal values changed my life as a parent.

It took me almost forty years to figure out that the goal in life is not to want more, it is to be more. It took me almost forty years to figure out that our time here on earth is limited, while money is not. I wish I could go back in time knowing that life just didn't have to be so hard. I wish I knew then what I know now, and I am sure my life would be radically different.

Let us be clear however, I don't want it to be different. I wouldn't be the person I am today or have the family I do, if my life's choices hadn't unfolded the way they did. Life is all about choices, and we make the best choices we can based on the information we have at the time.

If you have picked up this book, you have made a choice. A choice to dive into your relationship with your money, and a choice to explore something different. I applaud you for that choice. *Your Income. Your Life!* is a financial methodology created for the purpose of helping you become financially better. This methodology is based on the correlation between the lifestyle you want (Your Life) and the income you need to fund it (Your Income).

This book will provide you with the information you need to live your life according to the things that are important to YOU. The book will help you explore your current relationship with money, and how that relationship affects the other areas of your life. It will explore your relationship with money, and how it affects the world your kids are living in.

My goal is to provide you with the tools you need to change your financial landscape and create something different. It will give you the opportunity to instill a different set of values with your kids that stand the test of time. It will provide you with different information so you can make the choices that are right for your life. I will talk about the three situations most parents find themselves in, and give you simple and straightforward steps to improve your finances and model something better for your kids.

It is your income, and it is your life.

# CHAPTER 1

# YOU ARE NOT ALONE

Don't tell me what your priorities are. Show me where you spend your money and I'll tell you what they are.

James W. Frick

"Empty pockets never held anyone back. Only empty heads and empty hearts can do that."

Norman Vincent Peale

Do you feel like you are living paycheck to paycheck and still keep falling further behind? Are you making a good income, but still have a nagging feeling that you just can't get ahead? Each time you make more money, are you finding yourself with more commitments? Do you feel like you are being held captive by your job, and imprisoned by the hands that feed you? I can tell you, you aren't alone.

When I started to look at the data, I was shocked to see how many other parents out there were in a very similar situation to me. To be honest, I was a little relieved at first to know that I wasn't alone. Nevertheless, that feeling soon faded.

CHAPTER 1 - YOU ARE NOT ALONE

There are several studies that provide some startling figures about how modern day families manage their money. In particular, they examine our approaches to money, the use of financial products, and our financial habits. The research is similar regardless of what country you live in, however one in particular from Canada asked adults about their specific patterns of behaviour with money, and included a questions about their level of knowledge on the subject.[1]

They found that parents aged 30-45 had more debt, as compared to each dollar of income, than any other demographic. The higher the level of education these parents had, the more debt they held. In fact, dual income families making between $100-250k per year had the highest levels of debt, while claiming to have the highest level of personal finance knowledge.[2]

I dug further. Canada now has the highest debt relative to family income of all G7 countries, and the US is not far behind.[3] Sixty-five percent of the people with debt, have at least three or more types of consumer debt, and households with children make up half of this group. Over sixty percent of working adults indicate that they are living paycheck to paycheck, and thirty percent of them have nothing saved for retirement.[4]

---

1 Understanding Financial Capability in Canada, Analysis of the Canadian Financial Capability Survey, Date of publication: February 9, 2011. Steve McKay, University of Birmingham. Pg7

2 Statistics Canada, Canadian Financial Capability Survey (CFCS), 2009. www23.statcan.gc.ca/imdb-bmdi/document/5159_D2_T1_V1-eng.pdf

3 Financial Post. Outlook 2016. http://business.financialpost.com/investing/outlook-2016/canadians-household-debt-highest-in-g7-with-crunch-on-brink-of-historic-levels-pbo-warns

4 Understanding Financial Capability in Canada, Analysis of the Canadian Financial Capability Survey, Date of publication: February 9, 2011. Steve McKay, University of Birmingham. Pg7

It continues. Of the individuals that have made it to retirement age, forty-three percent still have debt to pay off, and almost all of those have debt when they do retire.[5]

I should also point out, that the projected retirement age for those currently under 45 is now 73.[6]

Call it an epidemic, or call it a lack of education, call it what you want. The outcome is the same, and it is the same in all of the G7 countries.

## PARENTING FINANCES

We have too many forms of debt, and we owe too much on that debt. We are approaching retirement in the wrong way. Any significant correction in housing prices would put most homeowners under water. It appears as though we have learned very little from the economic downturn in 2009.

Harris Interactive found that 57% of households today, do not have a budget.[7] Personal finances are still the leading cause of divorce in North America, and with the ease of access to credit, the trend is likely to continue.

*Why don't we have budgets? Why is money still a taboo subject at home, and why have we come to rely on debt to fund our lives?*

Because we were brought up in an era where parents

---

5  Understanding Financial Capability in Canada, Analysis of the Canadian Financial Capability Survey, Date of publication: February 9, 2011. Steve McKay, University of Birmingham. Pg7

6  Understanding Financial Capability in Canada, Analysis of the Canadian Financial Capability Survey, Date of publication: February 9, 2011. Steve McKay, University of Birmingham. Pg7

7  Harris Interactive. Harris Interactive Inc. Public Relations Research, "The 2009 Consumer Financial Literacy Survey Topline Report & Data Sheet". http://www.nfcc.org/newsroom/FinancialLiteracy/files/2009FinancialLiteracySurvey.pdf

sacrificed so that we could have a different life than they did. We were brought up in an era in which money wasn't talked about, because money wasn't available. And when you didn't have money, credit wasn't a viable option, because interest rates were too high. Instead you sacrificed.

Our parents didn't have to budget because cash was still king. You don't need a budget when your spending is limited by the amount of cash in your wallet. You know when you are going to run out, and you adjust. You sacrifice. That is how families budgeted thirty years ago.

Are we living the life our parents wanted us to live? No, likely not. You may have them fooled into thinking you do, or you may have them convinced that they just don't understand modern banking technology, but if you were like me, I know you aren't living the life our parents wanted.

Our parents had discipline and followed their budget. It was a written budget because it was literally written down on the back of envelopes or on a notepad by the phone. It was a working budget because they stuck to it; when they ran out of money, they stopped spending.

To make matters worse today, debt is available when we want it, and it is available on demand. It is at our fingertips, and we don't ever have to talk about it if we don't want to. We just spend.

Because technology has changed so much, and credit is so readily available, the way our parents managed finances is not the way people need to manage them today. Our parents assumed that cash would guide our decisions on money the same way it did theirs. They had no way of knowing that the values they were living by wouldn't work in the modern era. More importantly, the values they were trying to teach us actually have contributed to the behaviors we have today. They wanted us to have more, and boy do we ever have more. But we have it, because we can borrow for it.

Cash and checks are now a thing of the past. And when we can't hold it, we can't feel it. We aren't able to get any feedback on the significance of a purchase, because plastic doesn't have the same effect. I am afraid that our kids' generation won't even know what it looks like.

My wife recently took the kids for a family swim and the cost to get in was $13. She took a $20 bill out of her purse and attempted to pay with it. To her surprise (and shock), the young lady working the counter said:

"Don't you have a debit or credit card?"

"No, I have cash." My wife responded.

"Nobody pays with cash anymore. I don't even have change for you."

"You are telling me you can't change a $20 bill?" My wife replied.

"I guess I could go ask my manager." And she did.

How is it that in the modern era, cash has become the equivalent of the debit card 20 years ago? Vendors then wouldn't take debit because it was so infrequently used. I am worried for the future generations and it presents a whole new challenge to modern day parents. How will we prepare them for a world without real money?

You likely already know that the leading cause of divorce in North America is <u>still</u> personal finances. Money is like heart disease, it is hidden, and it creeps up on you, despite how healthy (or successful) you look to the outside world.

## CHAPTER 1 - YOU ARE NOT ALONE

Have you ever bought something and hid it from your spouse? I have.

Have you ever brought something home and told your spouse it cost less than it actually did? I have.

Have you ever watched your spouse spend money, and you felt like you couldn't tell them not to because you thought it would cause a huge fight? I have.

Have you ever created a budget that you were afraid to show your spouse? I have.

I am an accountant. I like numbers. I used to create a weekly budget that was a masterpiece. It rolled the ending balance into the opening balance automatically. Then every week, I would override the opening balance because we blew our brains out spending, and start again. I would do this, each and every week. And I never talked to my wife about it.

I took care of the personal finances in our house because I was an expert. I did it to make everyone else's life easier. I stressed over our escalating Visa and line of credit balances so that my family didn't have to. I spared them the conversations. I was such a great spouse and patted myself on the back often.

When we went on vacations, we spent like we were rock stars. We convinced ourselves, that if we were on vacation, we weren't going to spend our time worrying about money. We were there to have fun, and if we needed something, our Visa would cover it. I think we actually believed that the amount we spent was a reflection of how good of a time we had. In reality, we did that so we didn't have to communicate or make decisions while we were away. I didn't realize it until much later.

Couples today are emotionally detached from their spending. Credit is accessible and cheap to acquire, and the only time we talk about finances is when it is too late. We spend hours and days worrying about our financial future and feel overwhelming anxiety with the thought of mentioning a cost to our spouse.

Debit and credit cards are the modern day currency, and most times we ignore the monthly e-statement we receive from the banks. We are too busy communicating with our friends on Facebook feeds and congratulating them for their fancy new cars, kitchen Reno's, trips away, and family snapshots.

We are comparing ourselves to the best moments from other people's lives each and every day. This is how we communicate about money. It is through indirect means and the banks are loving it. Why? Because they have learned how to capitalize on it.

Even if you survive whatever money crisis you experience with your marriage still intact, what will your relationship look like with your spouse when you eventually do retire?

## IS IT TOO LATE?

For many of us, we won't know we are in trouble financially, until it's too late. Our spending is forcing us to work more and more, and the time we have with our kids is diminishing. In some cases, we are working so much that it is unhealthy. In other instances we are one leaky roof away from a crisis. Most of us won't know until it is already too late. We think we are providing the best for our kids, when in reality the only thing they want from us is our time. We are missing out on so many levels, and if we are lucky enough to be able to stop working before 73, we won't be able to do much because we have saved up so little.

Do we need to make a change? Probably. But what is it that needs to change? What will happen if we don't change?

Likely more of the same.

As I previously mentioned, we are on a path to retire much later in life, and when we do, we still won't have control over our money. We will spend our entire adult lives trading time for money, in hopes of eventually getting out of the rat race and enjoying what life we have left.

But how much life will you have left if you get there and you still have debt? How much life will you have if it doesn't happen until you are 73? And what will you have missed along the way?

Have we become so detached from our money that we are left dreaming about what could have been instead of planning for what could be? Will we be happy looking back at all those years where we traded our time for someone else to get rich? Will the things you purchased today, outweigh the time you lose in the later years of your life?

Most parents don't buy into the extreme money websites and books, because they feel like someone else is telling them how they should live their lives. Why should I have to live a life of sacrifice, keep my kids out of the activities their friends are doing, and by-pass vacations so that I can save for some future date?

We want the best for our kids, just like our parents wanted for us. We want our kids to be set-up for success. However, what if the desire to have more, is part of the problem in the first place?

In the next chapter, I will discuss the money messages we received while growing up, and the money messages we are receiving from modern society. I will look at the impact those messages have had on our spending habits as adults, and how changes in technology are affecting our financial situations as a whole.

# CHAPTER 2

# MONEY IS AN ACQUIRED TASTE

We grew up in an age where our parents sacrificed, and we sacrificed. They spent years trading their time for money, and being loyal to one or two companies. They took the safe route and saved for our education so that we could have a better life than what they did. They worked the same job so that they could retire after we completed our schooling. They spent 40 + years working to retire with a modest pension.

In fact, some of our parents are still saving more money in retirement, or delaying retirement in hopes of leaving us, or our grandkids, a bit of a nest egg.

Our parents bought used cars and drove them till they died. Our parents took us to McDonalds for dinner and let us get anything so long as it was a hamburger. Our parents spent time with us vacationing on the west coast (for me, that was known as the Great Lakes). They gave us all the opportunities we needed, without spoiling us with a ton of material things.

Our parents didn't necessarily talk to us about money and

how to manage it, they taught us that we needed to work hard to get it. They exposed us to jobs at young ages and told us we needed to save up for our education. They taught us to want an education so that we wouldn't have to sacrifice anymore. Cash was still king and communication wasn't required. No money meant no consumption.

Whether it was your first job out of college, or something in your late thirties, if you are like me, for the first time in your life you had money without something to save for. You had reached the destination that your parents so desperately wanted, and you had landed a job or been in a place of making more.

So you did what I did. You spent it.

You went out for expensive dinners, and took the extravagant vacations. You realized that making more meant you could borrow more. You now had leverage, and interest rates were low. You bought fancy cars, and took more extravagant vacations. You spent as if you were a rock star because for the first time in your life, you could.

And your parents? They looked at you and they were delighted that you were getting to experience the things they didn't. They had succeeded.

Or did they?

If material possessions are a sign of financial health, then yes, many of us succeeded. We have more than our parents did. We are making more money, and spending more money, than they imagined was possible. Our friends drive nice cars, live in nice houses, and take nice vacations. We compare highlight reels everyday on Facebook, and we spend more money as a result. We continued to work more hours and trade more time, so that we could climb higher up the corporate ladder and buy more stuff. We had to in order to continually compete.

We are living the lives our parents wanted for us. You hear the pride in your parents' voices when they talk to their friends about you. They brag about where you are at in your career and all the things you have to show for it.

Am I right?

What they don't know is that for the most part we have bought into the societal norms that have made banks in North America successful for so many years. What our parents taught us, banks have exploited. We have bought into the notion that they are advisors and are there to help us. And, we have lost sight of the fact that they are just salespeople. Salespeople that have told us it is easy to have everything your parents have always wanted for you.

Here are some popular slogans you may have come across (I have added my own words to illustrate):

- With credit "You are richer than you think."
- "Create your vacation sooner," whether you have the money or not.
- We are here to help you "...get a jump on the things you want. Your personal loan specialists."
- Need more credit, call us. "That's Banking Your Way!"
- Sign up for another credit card, "...if it fits in your wallet, it fits in your life."
- You don't need to save any money up, we have "...a loan for every lifestyle."
- "Visa Chip Technology. Added security for your everyday spending."

▶ Always wanted a BMW? "Borrow for the car you want."

Banks have now linked the achievement of our personal goals, to the personal loan products they offer. They have financial instruments that give you unlimited access to money you can use for whatever you want, whenever you want it.

Are YOU really richer than you think? Probably not. Do you deserve a vacation whether you have the money for it or not? Probably not. Do you really want to live now, and pay for your big lifestyle for years to come? Probably not.

Since when did items in our wallet define our lives? Should borrowing money on a daily basis define convenience? I think you see the point. The examples are endless.

The banks have led us to believe we don't need to wait to enjoy the things we want in life, because we can just borrow to get them today. We have gone beyond the old adage "the more we make, the more we spend," to a new modern day "the more we are going to make, the more we commit ourselves to spend." We must keep up to our friends' highlight reels, and have all the things our parents wanted for us.

Unfortunately, wanting us to have more than what they did, has not provided us with more happiness. Many are realizing that money doesn't buy happiness, it buys things. And things don't make us happy over the long run.

*"When your kids look back on their lives, they will remember the times you spent with them, not the things you bought them."*

When you look back on your life, what are the fondest memories you have? I am sure they have to do with your experiences, and the time you had with you parents and friends, not the things or toys you played with.

Our parents meant well, but technology and economic policy have thrown an ugly wrench into their plans. They didn't budget or talk about money, because they didn't have to, and unfortunately, wanting more wasn't the financial education we needed to prepare for the modern world.

Money messages are passed to kids in multiple ways. Sometimes these messages are directly communicated, sometimes they are implied, and sometimes they are transmitted through the act of observation. Looking back at the money messages we received, and the resulting behaviour, shows us that we need to be more intentional. Intentional about how we talk to our kids about money, how we talk with each other about money, and intentional about how we act with our money.

Our kids are watching, and our kids are learning.

There is no way to accurately predict how technology or economic policy will impact our kids' futures. The tools and instruments we use today to manage our finances may not be the tools and instruments that are available in 20 years.

What we need to do is create a whole new set of values that we practice, and preach. If we want our kids to be more, we need to model more. We need to start creating a healthy relationship with our money.

Today's parents are more involved then they have ever been in their kids' lives. We take our kids on playdates, we go to all their school plays, and we do their homework with them. In fact, we identify so deeply with our parenting role, we serve our kids. We feel like their mistakes are our mistakes as parents, so we fix them before they even happen. And if we can't fix the mistakes before they happen, we are right there to pick up the pieces afterwards.

We should be commended.

Instead of watching from a distance, today's parents are watching from above. We are hovering over our kids like a helicopter because we are so present in their lives. We no longer need rules of the house, because we are there to tell our kids what to do all the time anyways. We parent our kids at their current level of competency, which limits their ability to move to the next.

Think for a minute about what that means for their financial health and independence? How do we expect our kids to cope with the challenges of money when they aren't left to deal with the challenges of everyday life?

I saw an example of this very recently.

Young adults entering the workforce today are struggling to make their own financial decisions. They are relying on their parents to do it for them. You know, the parents that have multiple loans and zero balances in their investment accounts.

*"I wish my Mom was here to help me fill out this pension information, I have done enough 'adulting' for the week."*

This was a comment recently heard at the benefits orientation meeting at my work. A young lady was wishing that her Mom was at work with her, to tell her what to do with her pension information. Scary.

Our helicopter parenting has now limited our children's abilities to think for themselves. Instead of rules, we have questions. Instead of teaching our children to manage in the real world, we have taught them how to manage Mom & Dad.

If we are making their financial decisions for them and they are wrong, who do you think they will look to in order to bail them out?

We need to re-evaluate our method of serving and educating our kids. Our intentions are good, but the results may not be. It is up to us as parents to live a healthy financial lifestyle, and provide our kids with values that enable them to become independent and deal with the anxiety that will inevitably come with money.

Since 2007, things have changed a lot. On a global basis, retirement and pension funds have evaporated, people are losing their jobs at record rates, and most recently, countries are abandoning their chosen currencies. What used to be the safe route isn't any longer. Many of us that have been buying the fancy cars and expensive dinners put off saving for retirement because we were too busy living the extravagant life. The more we made, the more we spent—because material possessions are a sign of success.

Personal finance health is one of the very few things that we are not taught in school. It is also one of the very few things that are rarely talked about at home. We are taught physical fitness and exercise through gym class. We are taught sex education through schools, and in some cases—from our parents. We are taught many things, but one of the things we are definitely not taught is personal finances. Why? Perhaps money is a little taboo and has the ability to separate classes. Not because of actual wealth, but because of perceived wealth. Money comes with a sense of guilt. It comes with a sense of anxiety, and it comes with a sense of dependence on what other people think.

What we don't realize is everyone is thinking about themselves. Everyone is just like you and me. Everyone is so concerned about how you are perceiving them, they have no time to worry about perceiving you at all. While you are obsessed about looking good and keeping up, so is everyone else. It is a game of cat and mouse, and no one ever wins.

I came across this quote which really struck a chord with me:

"When you're 20 you care what everyone thinks, when you're 40 you stop caring what everyone thinks, when you're 60 you realize no one was ever thinking about you in the first place"

Unknown

It is time to stop competing with debt filled highlight reels. It is time to open up the lines of communication on financial health and financial wealth. It is time to be vulnerable and open to other people's views. It is time to start connecting to others based on open and honest communication. And it is through these connections, that I believe we will all find more happiness in our lives.

## WHAT WE MODEL, WE TEACH

It is our job as parents to communicate values to our kids in the ways in which they will understand them. And actions speak so much louder than words.

My kids are still young. Just a few years ago I would be play shopping with them in the basement and I remember asking them how they wanted to pay for all the items in their baskets. When they said "credit card," I thought it was so cute. They observed Mom and Dad paying for things with their credit cards, and they modelled it in their play.

Fast forward to today, after a year of using cash, our kids no longer give this same response. When I ask them how they will be paying, they say "cash." They even took the liberty to cut up a bunch of playing cards into small pieces, so that they would have the cash to buy the play food they wanted.

We model our values each and every day whether we know it or not. Often times, we find ourselves working hard and juggling tasks, because we are so invested in our career goals. What happens though, when those career goals are driven from the financial rewards associated with wanting more? We end up modelling the wrong values to our kids. We are showing them that work causes stress, and that work leaves us unsatisfied. Our actions are showing them that we must work harder to buy more things, even if that work takes us away from our family.

So many of us talk about the challenges in finding work life balance, and finding time to exercise or invest in ourselves. Perhaps it is because we haven't examined our personal and familial values, in relation to our financial values. Perhaps like me, you didn't really have financial values at all? Instead, your behaviors are driven from the societal pressures and your desire to have more, just like our parents wanted.

When you choose not to talk about money in front of your kids, they learn that money is taboo. When you show anxiety when talking about money, they see money as a source of stress. When you feel entitled to buy something on impulse, they see money as something they are entitled to. If you are never able to get control of your finances, they will struggle to control theirs.

Remember: how you model your life, will directly impact how they live theirs.

Financial literacy and education are not taught in schools. Everyone needs to find a way to learn financial values, and those values need to be reinforced each and every day. If you want your kids to have financial values which will guide them through life, you need to talk to them about those values. You need to live them. It is time to sit down with your spouse, and be honest about your current relationship with money. It is time to stop purchasing that feeling you are looking for.

You have the unique opportunity to take control over your financial health and instill values in your children that will help them achieve abundance in their lives. My goal is to provide my kids with the opportunity to **be more**, instead of having more. What's yours?

# CHAPTER 3

# UNDERSTANDING THE IMPACT OF DEBT ON OUR LIVES

Most modern day parents understand what they are supposed to do with their money, but struggle in how they do it. Most of us have children at a point in our lives, where debt has already become a normal part of our routine. And when children enter our lives, we do what every parent before us has done: we do more.

When we enter parenthood with a substantial amount of debt, the challenge to improve our financial health becomes more daunting. Modern-day parents have kids much later, well after they have established their careers and travelled to the places they didn't get to see growing up. Modern-day parents have learned through modern-day experience: to leverage their income and access the abundance of credit that is available to them.

We can hear our parents' voices each time we make yet another significant purchase. "Don't buy something if you don't have the money for it." Or if you are like me, you start rolling your eyes before your Dad can finish telling you that he "always saved up for a rainy day and paid cash for cars." You think, he just doesn't get it.

Times have changed. In the modern era, we don't need to save up because we make enough money that we can make all of our monthly payments with the income we have coming in. In the modern era, we don't have to worry about rising interest rates because the government knows it would stifle the economy as we know it. Times have changed.

We know what we are supposed to do with our money, and that is why we spend so much time justifying why we aren't doing what is right. To make matters worse, interest rates are low, so we believe we aren't paying much for our mistakes.

## THE COST OF DEBT

Including our houses, the typical modern-day family making over $100k per year, holds $350,000 in debt, across at least 3 different types of consumer loans. Here is a typical breakdown:

*Exhibit 1*

| Loan | Balance | Interest Rate | Minimum Payment | Term (years) | Annual Interest * | Total Interest |
|---|---|---|---|---|---|---|
| 1 Mortgage | $ 280,000 | 3.5% | $ 1,624 | 20 | $ 9,459 | $ 109,733 |
| 2 Car Loans | $ 50,000 | 5.0% | $ 805 | 6 | $ 2,259 | $ 7,978 |
| 3 Line of Credit | $ 11,000 | 4.0% | $ 203 | 5 | $ 489 | $ 1,155 |
| 4 Credit Cards | $ 9,000 | 20.0% | $ 834 | 1 | $ 1,005 | $ 1,005 |
| Total | $ 350,000 | | $ 3,466 | | $ 13,212 | $ 119,871 |

*Annual interest year 1

Do most parents understand just how much is paid in interest each year? Probably not. The average household in this demographic, is paying over $13,000 in interest each year. Over the life of those loans, almost $120,000 in interest.

Think about what that family could have bought for that $13,000 per year, if they hadn't given it to the bank. I can tell you that our parents thought about it!

We know that we aren't supposed to be financing our lives, but we do it anyways. Banks are legally required to show you, your annual cost of borrowing on any loan document. How many of us actually add up the amounts before we sign? I never did. One of the most common myths I hear often is "the banks wouldn't lend it to us if we couldn't afford it."

They will.

I lived my life in fear and with a scarcity mindset for many years. I didn't see what was right in front of me, and I spent money because I wanted what I thought others had and I borrowed to do it.

Unfortunately, this mentality limited my ability to communicate with my wife and be present for my family. I worked too much, and spent even more. I looked for comfort in all of the wrong things. It was much easier to appear successful, than figure out how to actually be successful. It was easier, because it was less work.

I would hide spending from my wife and avoid money conversations. I didn't want her to know that her accountant husband wasn't able to control our own finances. I didn't want her to know that we had so much debt it was straining our budget. I didn't want her to know that I was failing because I thought it made me look weak. We joked about the missed payments on the hydro bill and laughed off the visit from their collection agent. It was easier to tell her that I was busy at work, than admit what we were doing wrong. I was living a life in fear and it was killing me inside. It was no way to live.

We were eventually able to see debt for what it was, and create a new normal. You can too. And once you start to see the impact debt had on your life, you can then start to see your income differently as a result. You start to see the possibilities that are in front of you. You can start to plan properly for retirement.

## DEBT AND RETIREMENT PLANNING

I could see now, that the sooner I got rid of our debt, the sooner our cost of living drops, and the sooner retirement becomes a possibility.

The retirement age in North America has changed drastically over the past 20 years. For some, the enjoyment of working and the sense of purpose alone are driving them to work longer than people did in the past. For others, their financial health (or lack thereof) is driving them there.

We were taught to get a job, work 45 years, save, live frugal, invest, and then retire. If you are lucky, you will retire a little earlier because the stock market worked in your favor, and if you aren't so lucky, you will work a little longer because it worked against you. Alternatively, if you didn't follow your parents' lead, you have accumulated debt, and want to get it paid off before you leave your job for good.

Most of us don't really plan for retirement. We put a percentage away each year because we know that is what we are supposed to do. Or, we put a bit in at tax time because we realize that we under-contributed earlier in the year. We are too busy keeping up paying for our past (our debt) to worry about our future.

I was like this too, until I realized that I was overcomplicating things. I had bought into what banks and financial advisors were selling, and figured it was a complex formula that could wait for another day. I have come to figure out since, calculating your retirement number is actually pretty simple. It's your life, and it's your income. In order to figure out how much you need to have saved up, in order for you to be able to retire, in order to for you to stop trading your time for money, you need to figure out how much you want to live on.

From there, it's just math. It is:

Your cost of living, divided by the rate of return on your investments. In this sense, you are living off the annual return, and never withdrawing anything from the principle. It is passive income in its truest form.

## EXAMPLE

As a middle-aged parent, let's assume that you want to leave your kids a nice inheritance after your death, and you need to generate enough interest income each year to support your cost of life. Your entire nest egg will go to your kids.

If you were getting a 10% annual return (after tax), and have expenses of $50,000 per year, you would need $500,000 in your retirement fund to retire. This amount would hold true regardless of your age, as your income is entirely driven from your life.

If you were getting a 5% annual return, had $50,000 of expenses per year, you would need $1,000,000 in your retirement fund to retire.

For me, that number is not far off, given that 40% of our

current expenses are tied up in debt. If we can shed ourselves of the debt burden, we can significantly lower our retirement number. What about your parents? Are they over the age of 65 and still working? The math is similar for them.

If your parents were receiving a government pension plan or old age security, you would simply reduce the cost of their life by this amount. For example, in many countries the average person over the age of 65 receives $1,000 per month in government pension and/or old age security. Based on the scenario above, we would deduct this $12,000 from the individual's cost of living to figure out the amount of annual income they would require from their retirement savings account. In this case, they would need $380,000 in their account when yielding a 10% after tax rate of return.

So what happens if they want to be more conservative in their investments and only expect their annual rate of return (after tax) to be 5%? Simply divide their annual cost of living by the rate of return. In this case, it would be $760,000 ($38,000 / 0.05).

60% of the people that enter into retirement, do so without debt. Your parents are likely in that category. If so, they will have accumulated wealth in their retirement accounts, in their savings accounts, and in their house. Perhaps you can convince them that they don't need to keep that large inheritance, and that you would rather they spend this time enjoying life, and enjoying their grandkids. They could consider using up a portion of their investment each year and leaving you with less of that wealth. With the values you have, you probably won't need a big inheritance anyways. Your retirement calculation does get a little more complicated, but the principle is still simple.

They will need to draw down their investment at a rate that is equal to the number of years they need the money, less the interest earned. So the important variable becomes how many years they have, until they can live off of the government's pension and income supplement.

Let's use the numbers from before, and examine the numbers at different retirement ages, assuming we want to fund the same life we are living today, until we reach the age of 85. At that time, we will live off of our government pension, and our guaranteed income supplement.

*Exhibit 2*

| | Cost of Living | CPP/OAS | Income Required | Withdrawal Rate | Return | Retirement Fund |
|---|---|---|---|---|---|---|
| 60 | $ 50,000 | $ 6,600 | $ 43,400 | 6% | 5% | $ 642,261 |
| 65 | $ 50,000 | $ 12,000 | $ 38,000 | 6% | 5% | $ 497,242 |
| 70 | $ 50,000 | $ 16,800 | $ 33,200 | 6% | 5% | $ 361,835 |
| 73 | $ 50,000 | $ 16,800 | $ 33,200 | 6% | 5% | $ 308,973 |

I have factored in the reduced government income that they would receive if they decided to retire before 65, and the increased income if they retire after 65. As you can see, the amount required in your investment account is much lower the closer one gets to retirement age.

Let's say your parents are 67 years old and trying to figure out if they can retire. In order to live with $50,000 per year, you would need $407,499 in your retirement account, earning a 5% annual return. Want to live off of less? The amount drops again.

What is the cost of retirement in North America today? *MoneySense* magazine has indicated three different benchmarks that you can shoot for, and the annual cost of living under each.

## CHAPTER 3 - UNDERSTANDING THE IMPACT OF DEBT ON OUR LIVES

1. Bare bones retirement - $27,400
2. Middle class retirement - $51,000
3. Deluxe retirement - $100,000[8]

We are a family of five, living a very nice life, and our annual cost of living is below $60,000. Unless you have found significant financial health, and grown accustomed to an extravagant lifestyle, one likely doesn't need a deluxe retirement.

And if not, you just may be "richer than you think!" Talk to your investment advisor today.

As I mentioned early, retirement is changing. But it is hard to see. Perhaps you look at people the same way that I did. The ones that have retired early have done so because they were lucky, they had rich parents, or came into quick money.

Upon further reflection, you start to realize that you have always been easily impressed by material things other people have, and you spend money to try to compete. You have lived paycheck to paycheck your entire life, and assume that everyone else does as well. And unfortunately, after 20 years of saving, you have very little net worth and almost no money in the bank.

So what went wrong?

You had no plan and never defined for yourself what was important in life. Don't worry, it is not your fault, you simply did what your parents wanted you to do. You had more. You lived your life in direct comparison to your level of income, and supplemented that income with extensive levels of debt. And now that you have started to think about retirement, you think it is too late to retire and live the life you have grown accustomed to.

---

[8] http://www.moneysense.ca/save/retirement/retirement-three-magic-numbers/

What if you looked at the world through a different lens?

You can. Times are changing, and people are starting to adapt. People are starting to realize that you can live the life, and still be young. Old age is no longer the only path to wealth and retirement, and what used to be the safe route isn't so safe any longer. Trading your time for money is not the only solution to generating income, and the evolution in technology is proving that. More and more people are finding ways to reduce the cost of their lives, and are going out on their own. The internet is allowing people to create sales at a scale that was unheard of 20 years ago. They are working when they want to work, and on their own terms.

Do you have to take this new route in order to stop working earlier? You can, but you don't have to. It is your choice, and if you want to continue to trade your time for income, do so. Just know your numbers and work your plan. You will get there, in time.

# CHAPTER 4

# THAT MONEY FEELING

In order to understand how to be financially stable, we must first understand what money can, and cannot do for us.

The current reality is most of us will go through five or six career changes in our lifetime. If you think you are irreplaceable, you are not. If you think the company you are working for needs you, you are likely wrong. There is someone who needs you, and someone that thinks you are irreplaceable though. Your family. Therefore, you have a choice to make.

You can continue to work more and spend more, to make up for the time you are away from your kids. You can continue to compete with your friends and buy more stuff for gratification. You can continue to do the things you have in the past, and get similar results.

Or, on the other hand, you can decide to do something different. You can decide to take back control of your finances, get on the same page as your spouse, and recognize that time is so much more precious than money.

The reality is, there are many well-paid parents who are miserable, and their misery has nothing to do with the amount of income they have. It has to do with the fact that their money controls them. They have no freedom, because they are stressed in their job and are working so much that they are never home to strengthen the relationships they have with their spouse or their kids.

We operate as if money is the goal and we do it at the expense of the three things that matter most in our lives: our family, our health, and our freedom. Those three things drive our happiness, and happiness is the wealth we are really seeking.

If you are operating the same way I was, you lack wealth because you are misusing your money. Instead of your money buying freedom, it is buying you things that you associate with wealth. You see what others have, and believe that those things bring respect and joy. You want others to respect and admire you. You use your money and get an immediate feeling of gratification, only to find that it passes in time along with that feeling of happiness. And when it comes to your kids, you are buying them things, instead of experiences.

When that initial feeling of happiness passes, you find yourself having to work more so that you can do it all over again. In the end, the more you buy, the less freedom you have, and that lack of freedom is affecting your health. It is distancing your from your family. When your level of spending exceeds the money you have coming in, the hand that feeds you binds you. You work so that you have income, your income funds the lifestyle you think you want, your lifestyle forces you into debt, and you must work harder to do it all over again. In essence, your money has imprisoned you.

We need to realize wealth does not come from the amount of money we have, it comes from the value that money brings.

What we seek is not money itself; it is the freedom to do what we want, when we want to do it. The freedom to be present for your kids and watch them grow up. The freedom to pursue our dreams, and help other people without the financial burden that is associated with it. What we want is the freedom to create the life we are destined to live.

## WHAT YOU SEEK IS CLOSER THAN YOU THINK

What if I told you your income doesn't have to define your lifestyle and you can take back control over your personal health and well-being? Would you be interested?

What if I told you that you didn't need to feel like you were throwing your life away in hopes of something better? Would you be interested?

I bet you would.

It is your choice. You can, and will, decide how much debt you want to live with, and how you want to live your life.

Before we get into *how* to improve your relationship with money, let me make some arguments for *why*. Yes, our struggles are slightly different, but the freedom we seek, and the role that money plays, is the same. Each one of us has a relationship with money, and that relationship is all about choice.

When you are living in darkness because of your finances, it is the hardest time to see the light. By investing in myself, I started to recognize all of the things that were right in front of me all along. I saw the abundance I had in my life, and I became grateful for it. In addition, the more I saw, the more grateful I became. It was no longer a feeling of guilt and shame for what I didn't have, it was a feeling of pride and joy for all the things I did.

## CHAPTER 4 - THAT MONEY FEELING

We have a choice in our lives. We can approach our money from a victim mindset, or we can approach it from a mindset based on gratitude. A guest by the name of John O'Leary said it best on the *Good Dad Podcast*. He has an amazing book called *On Fire* that I highly recommend as well!

He said:

"Your perception of your life can be totally different based on how you ask yourself three important questions.

1. Why me?
2. Who cares?
3. What can I do about it?"

John explains that the victim asks these questions from a defeated mindset.

First Question. Why me? Poor me. Why don't I have the ability to have the things that that person does?

Second question. Who cares? I can't make the money that person does, so who cares? I can't live off less, so why should I care?

Third question. What more can I do? I didn't have the opportunities that person did, so there is nothing more I can do to make this situation better.

Then he explains how a person looks at these questions from a gratitude mindset.

First Question. Why me? Why am I so lucky? Why am I so blessed? Why do I get the chance to do this again tomorrow, when I messed up so much today?

Second Question. Who cares? Who cares if it is hard? Who cares if it is going to take time? Get over it. I can do better today than I did yesterday, so who cares?

Third Question. What more can I do? What can I do to ensure tomorrow is better than it was today? What can I do to make sure my kids don't make the same mistakes I did? What can I do to help others, have a little bit, of what I have?

Instead of looking at our life with a sense of scarcity, we can make a choice to look at it with a sense of abundance. We have everything we need in life right in front of us if we take the time to see it. In reality, what we need more of, is time.

My hope is that the *Your Income. Your Life!* methodology can help you see that you have an opportunity to be more. It has done that for us, and for the first time in my adult life, I feel like I am living the life I was destined to live.

# CHAPTER 5

# YOUR TRUE COST OF LIVING

My income was about to change, whether I liked it or not. We needed to lower our cost of living, if we were going to keep the possessions we valued, and weather the coming storm.

You may be wondering how we ended up with so much debt, and whether or not this was something we had experienced before. Unfortunately we had, and as too many people have come to learn, it isn't that hard to rack up a substantial amount of debt in a relatively short period of time.

Fifty percent of my compensation was paid through bonuses, and every four months I would have a large check to deposit at the bank. In between these bonus checks, we would borrow from one of our three lines of credit, and pay the monthly interest. We would pay our lines of credit off and the repeat the process all over again.

The problem at this point in time, was that we had grown so accustomed to those large bonus checks that we didn't hesitate to splurge on items for our brand new house. We bought a vinyl fence, we put a stamped concrete driveway in, we had our landscaping professionally done, and we even put in remote control blinds.

We had racked up debt on all three of our lines of credit, only to see that the bonus checks were about to run dry. In the introduction, I mentioned that budgeting probably saved our lives. In reality, it wasn't the budget itself that saved us, it was the calculations that I started to do as a result of that budget, and the realization that we needed to change our behaviors, fast.

We sat down, reviewed our budget together, and knocked out a plan. We immediately started to take a percentage of each paycheck, and had it automatically pay down our lowest balance line of credit. In addition, when that next bonus check came, we put 100% of it into our debt. Within nine months, we had made substantial progress!

Here is where it gets interesting. After creating a newfound discipline in our life, and opening the doors of communication on our spending, I realized the opportunity that was in front of me all along.

I didn't need the stressful job I had relied on for so long. I didn't need to get yelled at by our VP anymore. By changing the cost of our life, we had changed the amount of income we needed to live it. More importantly, we hadn't sacrificed anything in the process. We were still doing the things we wanted to do, taking vacations when we wanted to take them, and feeling better the whole time.

I had just shattered the myth that I was living under my entire adult life. My income didn't have to drive my life! The things that I wanted access to, were available to me all along, and the only reason I didn't see it was because we kept spending our money before we earned it. We lacked the patience to wait until money came in, because I was the budget guy at home, and at work. When I saw that there was a $30,000 bonus check coming, we spent it before I had even submitted that forecast to head office. I was going to make more, so we spent more.

In 2014, our debt equalled 40% of our after-tax income. This meant that the true cost of our "living" expenses was only 60% of the income we were bringing in. This was the first time I had ever looked at it this way. It seemed so very simple. I had been spending almost as much on things we didn't each year, as we were spending on things we did. Moreover, I struggled to figure out where we had spent it each and every time!

From there, I started to examine many things about my relationship with money, and started to question the things I had overlooked for too long.

Would I look back in 20 years and be happy about how many hours I spent at work? Would I look back and be happy about the time I spent away from my kids? Would I be ok with the fact that I wasn't present, even when I was home with my family?

Moreover, my lack of patience from the guilt I had built up inside; what would that do to my kids' behaviors as they got older? Would I even be here in 20 years to look back, based on the increasing level of stress I was experiencing?

Was all of this worth the money that we were over-spending each year? The stress of making more, so we could spend more on things we struggled to identify. Was it really worth it?

I started to read more and more on personal finances and felt a renewed passion as an accountant. I went to work on spreadsheets and started to figure out what possibilities were laying right in front of me that I had never imagined. I had been working under the methodology that I had to have enough in retirement to fund my current level of expenses. Why? Because that is what we were told to do.

After I realized where the extra spending were going, I started to look at the rest of our debt as well. What if we could live the same way we were, without any debt at all? How much would the cost of our life be then? How much would I need in income if we had no payments to make to the banks? It looked something like this:

*Exhibit 4*

| Category | | Amount | |
|---|---|---|---|
| Investments | $ | 10,000 | |
| Debt Payments | $ | 35,000 | |
| Committed Costs | $ | 25,000 | |
| Cash Costs | $ | 10,000 | |
| Mystery Expense | $ | 5,000 | |
| Savings | $ | - | |
| **TOTAL CASH OUT** | $ | 85,000 | Your Life' |

I could take our cost of living down from $85k, to about $50k. I was astonished. Even if I add back $10k per year to put into our savings accounts in order to fund the things that come up in life, our cost of living was only $60k.

I didn't need to keep working in a job that made me miserable after all. Moreover, I would need a lot less money when I wanted to retire!

I didn't stop there. I then started to explore how much of our committed costs were truly committed, and how much of our mystery expenses were really a mystery. I looked at all the stuff we have stored in the basement and started to see opportunities instead of work. If we could instill a level of discipline and curb our consumption calories, we could change our financial picture, fast. The possibility of being home and available to my family wasn't so far out of reach after all.

Sure, I can make arguments for investing instead of paying down my debt based on the interest differential. The piece of the puzzle I was missing, was the impact that my mortgage payments were having on the life I wanted to live. I had to make the money I was making, in order to fund the commitments I made in the past. This level of funding was driving the amount I had to make, and the time I would have to keep making it. I also figured I would have to keep making those similar monthly payments for many years, because I would have done what I always did. I would have replaced one eliminated payment with a new one. I would focus on what I should pay monthly, instead of what I could do monthly.

I had made a huge revelation in how I wanted to live my life going forward.

# CHAPTER 6

# LIVING LIFE ON YOUR OWN TERMS

*Your Income. Your Life!* is a financial methodology I discovered as way of helping other parents become financially responsible. The words describe finances as a relationship between the lifestyle you want (Your Life) and the income you need to fund it (Your Income).

I recognized that many parents in the modern era were in a similar situation as we were. We had an unhealthy relationship with money, but weren't on the verge of a crisis. We had put some of the pieces of the financial puzzle in place that would help us in the future, but deep down, we knew there were other areas holding us back. We needed a path to something better, but we didn't need a total money makeover. We wanted a methodology that would allow us to create the life we wanted, regardless of our income, and we wanted it fast.

## THE SIMPLE MATH

Your Income:

- Income earned through paycheck
- Income earned through investments
- Income earned through the sale of stuff

Your Life:

1. Costs you have committed to:
   - debt
   - property taxes
   - leases
   - subscriptions
   - memberships
   - bills
2. And Other Costs (I like to call cash costs):
   - groceries
   - transportation
   - gifts
   - vacations
   - entertainment
   - maintenance & repairs

The difference between your income, and your life, is your net cash flow. If you want to improve your finances, you have a choice based on the lifestyle you want. You can:

1. Increase your income
2. Lower your committed costs
3. Lower your cash costs

The goal? You want to create as much separation as possible between your income, and the cost of your life, so that you can start improving your financial landscape and accumulating wealth. This positive cash flow is used to pay off your debt, and increase your investments. We will explore all of the steps you can take to impact upon these three items later. What is important for now, is to realize that eventually, your money can work harder and provide more for you, than your job will.

In order to adopt this methodology though, you must first take a long hard look in the mirror. You need to look at what you have been taught through your upbringing, from society, from the media, and from banks. You need to accept the fact that the things you have bought into, are all garbage. They are not serving you and feeding you the happiness you seek. Money does not define success, and won't bring you happiness. Happiness must come from within. You need to realize that wealth can't be purchased through a monthly payment, but rather, it comes from the values we live by and the abundance we surround ourselves with. It comes from making real human connections. Moreover, if you ever want to be able to make real connections with people, you need to make a real connection with yourself first.

## BE HONEST ABOUT YOUR RELATIONSHIP WITH MONEY

If you really knew as much as you pretend to about finances, you wouldn't be in the situation you are today. You wouldn't be struggling to keep up, or struggling to get ahead. You would already be debt free, accumulating wealth, and focused on retirement. You would have asked for the help you needed, and you would be focused on becoming better. Both personally and financially.

It is in our times of failure that we often see the most growth. It is time to accept your past failures, and be real about the failures we will experience in the future. It is time to reach out to people and educate yourself on money in the modern era. It is time to create a relentless desire to be better tomorrow, than you are today. If you want to be better as a parent, and as a spouse, it is time to start talking about your finances.

Start today, and take an inventory of where you stand financially. Be honest with yourself, so that you can start being honest with those around you. When you are honest with yourself about where you are failing, you will be ready for others to be honest with you in return. If you are in debt, admit it. If you are living paycheck to paycheck, that's OK. If you can't afford to do something because you want to live within your means, learn to say no. People will respect you more when you are honest with them, than they will if you go along with something you didn't want to, and resent them for it.

Focus on all of the behaviors you have with money that are hurting you. Not the behaviours of your spouse or your kids. The behaviours that *you* have developed, in your adult lifetime, that are holding you back from financial stability. The behaviours that are holding you back from financial improvement. The behaviours, that are holding you back from accumulating wealth and creating the freedom you seek.

The amazing thing is, it is never too late. Once you are honest with yourself, and make a decision to do something different, the path to financial freedom is a lot closer than you think.

Make the decision and start listening to people about their experiences with money, so that you can learn from them. Listen to learn and communicate, instead of listening to be heard. There is value in every message we receive, so long as we receive it with an open mind. I have learned that power comes not from the strength we exhibit; it comes from the humility we possess.

It's *Your Income, and it's Your Life*. Start living it on your own damn terms! If you can lower the cost of your life, you can lower the amount of income you need to make. If you can lower the amount of income you need to make, you will free up time to start investing in yourself. When you invest in yourself, the things you do for others will be better as a result. Stress will dissipate, and with a lower income requirement, the time you need until retirement will drop too. This simple methodology helped me realize the steps I needed to take to change the trajectory of my future.

Whether you are looking to take back control of your finances, re-define your relationship with money, or accelerate your plans for retirement, this methodology can help you. It isn't just about the numbers, it is about creating a set of values that will allow you, to live your life, on your own terms! It is about accepting and letting go of the past, so you can build on your strengths and create more for the future.

## ALIGNING YOUR FAMILY VALUES WITH YOUR FINANCIAL VALUES

The Oxford Dictionary defines family values as:

> "values held to be learned or reinforced within a family, such as those of high moral standards and discipline"

The values you have in your home, are passed from generation to generation. If you want your kids to be more, you need to instill values in them that allow them to be more. In order to instill values in your kids, you need to model those behaviours as adults. You need to show them that you can follow the standards you set have set for yourself, and create the life you want to live.

Anyone can create a budget. Anyone can save up a thousand dollars for a rainy day. Anyone can calculate how much income they need to have in order to fund the life they want to live. That is just math.

Where we struggle is in discipline and in communication. We struggle with the most important steps on our path to financial freedom. We struggle to talk with our spouses and our family about what matters most in our lives, and how we financially want to live them. Every single parent I have counselled about money, has told me that talking to their spouse was the hardest part. Many have worked through the numbers, and figured out that something needed to change, but almost everyone struggled to have the conversation they needed to have in order to facilitate a change.

We realized that we needed to create some values that would help us approach our money differently than we had in the past.

## OUR VALUES

- We will not let our money control us, we will control it.
- We will involve everyone in our family in money decisions.
- We will talk about what we need, before we buy it.
- We use cash to pay for anything that loses value.
- We will reward ourselves for progress.

Once we starting applying these values, we started to see the messages in society for what they are, and started making different choices based on what was right for us. It amazed us that we could include our kids in our decisions at four and five years old, and they had the ability to contribute a lot. Finally, we realized that banks were not our allies, and just because it "fits in our wallet" does not mean it should fit in our life.

Is it easy to live based on these values? Not always. Some days are harder than others. But it is so much better than when we had none. Instead of feeling like we are living a life of sacrifice, these values allow us to live our life. Moreover, these values are helping us with more than just money. These values are helping us make better decisions about the food we eat, the conversations we have, and the time we spend together.

# CHAPTER 7

# TIME IS MORE IMPORTANT THAN THINGS

As you have now learned, I have made many mistakes with money over the years. I knew the importance of a budget, yet I would let months go by without updating ours. I borrowed money to buy things that lost value, I spent money on things without consulting with my spouse, and I spent money on things that I hid from my spouse. Most importantly, I did these things knowing I would have to work harder, and spend time away from my family, just to pay them off.

That was my life and I felt like I had little power to change it. I woke up each day and asked myself why? Why was it so hard for me when it seemed so easy for others? Why couldn't I have financial freedom so that I didn't have to spend so much time away from my family? Why me?

I felt like there was nothing I could do to change my situation.

When I finally decided to get serious about my finances, I started reviewing every charge on our Visa and every withdrawal from our bank. I needed to know exactly where our money had gone, if we wanted to be able to make decisions on where it should go in the future.

It was eye-opening for us, and it worked, because we talked about our spending without judgement.

I have always had an idea how much my income was, and how much my life costs. Nevertheless, it still didn't stop me from overspending. Why? Because personal finance is not a mathematical equation. You need more than a budget on paper; you need a working budget. You need a budget that drives discipline, and discipline which changes your behaviour.

If you want to live within your means, you need to spend less each month than what you make. Create positive cash flow.

I know that it is easy to say, and much harder to implement. The important thing though, is that you need to implement it. Create a viable plan, and act on that plan immediately.

For years, I told myself that the complex budget model I had created was a working budget, but now I clearly see that it wasn't. I had created my own little shell game, and the only winner was the bank.

If we wanted to control our money, we needed to have a budget model that was simple enough for everyone in our family to understand. It needed to cover a set period of time, and it needed to be a fixed target. One month's failures could not be carried forward to the next month's budget. If we were to control our money, we needed a budget that worked every month. Our income, had to cover our life.

Back in 2014 when we faced a sudden drop in income, that budget model helped saved my life. My wife and I went to work examining our spending, and we agreed that our debt had to go, and it had to go right away. With the excess cash flow we had coming in, we set up recurring payments well in excess of our minimum payments, and in just 9 months we were able to pay off everything, with the exception of our vehicle loans. It was remarkable, but I was still not seeing what was right in front of me all along. Not until I left my job.

I worked in the automotive industry for several years with 70-hour work weeks being the norm. I missed important things that my kids did because I was at work trying to make more for our family. One event in particular changed me as a leader, as a husband, and as a father. When I look back, this event started the journey that I am still on today.

It was 2011 and we were going through a terrible launch at work. Just one year earlier, I had been promoted to the Assistant General Manager, and I was now faced with a customer shutdown. Our new equipment wasn't able to keep up with the customer demand, and we had shut down General Motors. I worked 24 hours a day for 6 days straight. 18 hours in the plant, and 6 hours at home answering phone calls while I tried to sleep. The following Thursday night, I spent 27 hours in the plant before returning home to get some much-needed rest. It was 7am in the morning.

I woke up around 11:30am and felt an overwhelming sense of failure. I didn't want to get out of bed, but I had to. I remember walking downstairs and sitting on the couch next to my wife. When she reached around to give me a hug, I broke out in tears. I cried uncontrollably for several minutes.

"I have no idea what to do. I wish they would just fire me," I said to her. The question she asked next took me by surprise.

## CHAPTER 7 - TIME IS MORE IMPORTANT THAN THINGS

She looked back and asked "Are you doing what you think is right?"

I looked at her, and slowly said "yes."

It was as if she knew exactly what I needed to hear, when she replied:

"I trust you. If you are doing what is right, I trust that you will figure it out."

We did figure it out. But most importantly, through that time in my life, I figured out that my life was not defined by how I earned my income, it was defined by how I lived my life and the people that were in it.

I knew our kids were growing up whether I was there or not, and it frustrated me a lot.

When I finally made the decision to leave the job I always thought I wanted, I knew I was going to take a hefty pay cut. My wife and I had already concluded that we were not willing to move, and getting a different job in the same area, at the level I was making before, was very unlikely. We valued our home and our neighbourhood, and we valued having our parents and siblings close by. Moving just wasn't something we were going to consider.

So how could I take such a huge step? How could I take such a huge risk with three kids at home? I made the decision to leave because I had to. I didn't want to feel trapped any longer. I wanted to be present for my kids. Present physically when they had school plays and concerts, and present mentally when I there as well.

We had paid down a ton of debt and lowered our cost of living. With discipline and communication, and by living our financial values, we knew we could live a life of abundance on less income.

I spent the next 9 months with my family making up for lost time. I was able to drop our oldest off for her first day of kindergarten and pick her up at the end of the day. I was able to watch our youngest learn to talk and communicate with the world around her. I was able to see how much work went into raising kids, and how special the bond is that is created when you do so.

When I finally had that time with my kids, I started looking at my life through a different lens. I started to ask the same questions I did before, but from a very new perspective. I started to recognize and acknowledge the things in life that I was grateful for. My beautiful wife, three healthy kids, loving parents, and loving in-laws, a wonderful house in a great neighborhood, and friends that cared about me.

Why me? Why was I so lucky to have all these things in my life? Why did we have so few struggles when others had so many? Why were we so happy while others weren't?

With this new perspective, I saw that I did have the power to change my situation. Instead of convincing myself I couldn't change things in my life, I started to seek out ways to change them. What can I do to make things better? How can I make today better than yesterday? How can I make tomorrow better than today?

When you change the way you look at the world, you change the way you interact with the world. Not only that, when you are a parent, each change you make has an immediate impact on how your kids interact with the world. Your values around family and finances will drive your kid's values around family and finances too.

When I finally starting seeing that I already had all the important things that I was looking for in my life, I was able to see that my income shouldn't drive my life. Sure, money bought things, and those things gratified me. That gratification however, would always fade, and the things that I found myself grateful for, had nothing to do with money. It was the love of my spouse, and the love of my kids that mattered. It was the home that we would raise them in, and the support system we had built around it, which truly mattered.

I had finally realized that our time on Earth is limited and we have to make the best of it. Money is abundant; time is not. Everything I do is aimed at freeing up time so that I can be there for my family. Sure, I make a lot less today than I did before. However, I see my kids in the mornings and I eat dinner with them at night. I get to go to their school plays and camp concerts, and I know what really matters in my life. When I leave work, I leave my work. Moreover, when I am at home, I am mentally at home. Time is what I seek, and I want to model this every day I can with my kids.

My hope is that by modelling a different set of values, our behaviours will show our kids that family really does come first. We will strive to free up our time so that we can spend it with those we love, we will talk openly about how we manage our money in a way that helps us spend our time together, and we will control our finances so they don't end up controlling us.

# CHAPTER 8

# BUDGETING FOR A PARENT'S LIFE

In my personal coaching, I am often surprised how many people can't tell me how much money they make in a year. Perhaps they don't want to tell me how much they make because money is still so taboo, or perhaps it is because they truly don't know. Nevertheless, each time I get this answer, I can guarantee one of two things:

1. If you don't know how much you are making, you likely don't know how much you are spending
2. If you don't know how much you are spending, you likely don't have a working budget

If you want to improve your family finances, you need to know your numbers. It is that simple. If you don't know how much you are making (before and after tax), and how much you are spending every single month, you won't have the ability to improve.

A goal without a plan, is just a wish.

Antoine de Saint-Exupery

The budget is the foundation that financial stability, financial improvement, and financial growth depend on. It is your roadmap to something better.

## CREATE A BUDGET THAT WORKS

The budget needs to cover a few key things. Your monthly income, your monthly commitments, and your monthly plan for spending on all other items. Within your commitments, you will also need to understand your current relationship with debt.

You can find the *Your Income, Your Life* budget tool at www.YourIncomeYourLife/Resources, and it is free to download and use. I have broken it down into a series of steps that will help you populate your monthly budget plan, which you can print and share with your spouse.

You need a budget. If this tool doesn't work for you, create your own or find another free one online. In the modern era, everything is happening at lightning speed. Automatic withdrawals, electronic payments, email transfers, and debit and credit card transactions happen when we are busy at work. If you want to keep on top of it, you need to track it.

The first time my wife and I sat down together to figure out how much we were spending each month, we went back six months and reviewed every single transaction. I recommend you do so as well. We were in a situation where we needed to find ways we could reduce our life expenses.

This process not only helped us find ways to cut costs, it helped us instill a level of discipline that we would have never achieved before.

## YOUR INCOME

We all have three main sources of income in our lives. Active income, passive income, and liquidation income. Active income comes in the form of trading our time for money. We get paid based on the hours we work. Whether or not we are working for ourselves, or trading our time for the benefit of someone else, it is still active income. We must work for it, and it usually shows up in the form of a paycheck, a bonus, or a withdrawal from your company. As parents, it sometimes shows up as a child tax benefit as well, but that will depend on your level of annual income.

Passive income comes in the form of a return on effort you put in previously. Interest earned on money you invested, royalties from writing a book, or the sale of a training course you developed and are selling online. We are getting money for work we did in the past.

The third form of income comes in the form of selling things. You can sell possessions that you have accumulated over time, and the difference between what you sell it for, and what you owe on it, is your income. Here is a snapshot of the income section of our budget tool.

| YOUR INCOME | | | MONTH 1 |
|---|---|---|---|
| Paycheck 1 | Label | $ | - |
| Paycheck 2 | Label | | |
| One time payment | Label | | |
| Passive Income | Label | | |
| Disposal Income | Label | | |
| Other Income | Label | | |
| + Add item | Label | | |
| *INCOME AVAILABLE FOR YOUR LIFE* | | $ | - |

CHAPTER 8 - BUDGETING FOR A PARENT'S LIFE

## YOUR MONTHLY COMMITMENTS

Your monthly commitments show up in the form of regular payments, or automatic withdrawals. These commitments are fixed in cost each month, and are something you signed in the form of a contract. It can also be something you signed up for online, and if it varies in amount, that amount is based on seasonality or usage only.

You should be able to look at your bank account and your credit card statement to see which charges show up every month. Here is a snapshot of the items we have outlined in our Budget tool, excluding your committed debt payments.

| COMMITTED COSTS | | MONTH 1 |
|---|---|---|
| Life Insurance | Label | |
| Property Taxes | Label | |
| House Insurance | Label | |
| Electricity | Label | |
| Water | Label | |
| Cable TV | Label | |
| Internet | Label | |
| Phone | Label | |
| Cell Phones | Label | |
| Auto Gas/Oil/Service | Label | |
| Auto Insurance | Label | |
| Childcare | Label | |
| Tuition | Label | |
| Subscriptions | Label | |
| Gym Membership | Label | |
| Household service | Label | |
| Other | Label | |
| + Add item | Label | |
| | COMMITTED COSTS $ | - |

## CASH COSTS

We now use cash to pay for anything in our budget that isn't already committed, with the exception of items we have to order online, and gas for our vehicles. This was the hardest thing to implement, but the one thing that paid the most in return. When we started using cash to buy things, we started to appreciate the value of what we were paying for. Before we used cash, we didn't even pay attention to the prices we were paying for most things. We needed it, so we bought it. There was absolutely no association with the amount of money we had given up when the transaction went through at the cash register.

There is a reason that retailers are willing to pay a fee to Visa and MasterCard; they know that customers spend a significantly higher amount when they don't pay with cash. As consumers, we don't identify with the money that is changing hands, because there is no money changing hands. When you are using credit, you don't have to make a decision on the worth of an item until the end of the month when you look at your statement. When you spend your hard earned cash, you have to make that decision on the spot.

I compare it to the pain associated with a great workout. The next day you feel pain and you get immediate feedback on the success of your exercise from the day before. When you pay with cash, you get the same instant feedback, and that same good pain feeling. You know you were physically giving something up in order to get something in return, and you made a conscious decision at the time. Would you keep exercising if you didn't get feedback for 30 days? You might, but I guarantee, the exercise for those 30 days wouldn't be nearly as rewarding, if you didn't know it was working.

We don't use an envelope system to allocate money to certain things. Our budget does this for us. We know how much cash we have available, and we watch it disappear as the month progresses. We can see and feel our money, and that is the best

## CHAPTER 8 - BUDGETING FOR A PARENT'S LIFE

feedback we can ask for. It has saved us $700 a month on our cash costs, and thousands more on items that we would have purchased before when using credit.

Here is what we have identified in our cash costs:

| CASH COSTS | | | MONTH 1 |
|---|---|---|---|
| Groceries | Label | | |
| Clothing | Label | | |
| Sports & Entertainment | Label | | |
| Restaurants | Label | | |
| Pet Care | Label | | |
| Trips | Label | | |
| Birthdays | Label | | |
| Anniversary | Label | | |
| Christmas | Label | | |
| Gifts | Label | | |
| Kids Activities | Label | | |
| Other | Label | | |
| + Add item | Label | | |
| + Add item | Label | | |
| + Add item | Label | | |
| | | CASH COSTS $ | - |

## DEBT

The only area left to account for in our budget, is our debt. These are committed costs in that you have a minimum monthly payment, but I like to take it a step further and classify our debt into two different categories, good debt and bad debt. Then I like to keep them separate from the rest of our living expenses.

Find out all the forms of personal debt you have in your life, and write down the amount owing for each and every one. List out the type of loan you have, the minimum payment, the amount owing, and the number of months remaining. We will come back to that later. For now, it is important to see the minimum payments in your budget, so that we can see how much of our life we have committed to the banks.

Here is what it debt looks like in our budgeting tool:

| GOOD DEBT | | | MONTH 1 |
|---|---|---|---|
| Mortgage 1 | Label | | |
| Mortgage 2 | Label | | |
| Other | Label | | |
| + Add item | Label | | |
| | | GOOD DEBT $ | - |

| BAD DEBT | | | MONTH 1 |
|---|---|---|---|
| Car Loan 1 | Label | | |
| Car Loan 2 | Label | | |
| Car Loan 3 | Label | | |
| HELOC | Label | | |
| LOC | Label | | |
| Personal Loan 1 | Label | | |
| Personal Loan 2 | Label | | |
| Credit Card 1 | Label | | |
| Credit Card 2 | Label | | |
| Other | Label | | |
| + Add item | Label | | |
| | | BAD DEBT $ | - |

## NET CASH FLOW

Once you have populated all of your income and expenses, you will have a clear idea of what you have left over. If you are spending more than you make, you will see a negative net cash flow. If you are living within your means already, the net result will be positive.

This is where I caution most families. Take the time to go back six months, and review all of your mystery expenses. Get an accurate picture of how much your life has been costing you, so that you have a fighting chance moving forward. If you underestimate your expenses at this stage, you will set yourself behind in the process, several months.

Remember, it is time to be honest about what your relationship with money is, so that you can accurately define what you want it to be going forward. This is not time to judge your spending, it is time to acknowledge it.

Here is what the net number shows up as in our template:

| AVAILABLE FOR DEBT / SAVING / OR INVESTING | $ | - |
|---|---|---|

## THE FIRST BUDGET MEETING – GETTING ON THE SAME PAGE

Money is taboo in modern society. We didn't talk about money growing up because there wasn't money to talk about. Our parents lived a life of discipline and sacrifice, because they had to. Interest rates were high, and credit was hard to come by.

Our parents modelled the values they thought we needed, but they didn't talk to us about money. Their response to money questions was a universal:

"Do you think money grows on trees?"

Then they told us that we had to work hard to get money, and the harder we worked, the more we would have. We grew up with these financial values.

It is no surprise then, that when we worked hard and got more money, we spent more money. When interest rates plummeted and banks became lending factories, we borrowed so we could have even more. We convinced ourselves our parents couldn't borrow like us, because they didn't have the level of income we do today. We worked hard to get to this level, and by golly, we deserve to spend it. We are doing exactly as our parents taught us. However, when we need more, we end up working more.

Our parents did nothing wrong. They modelled the right behaviours! What they missed however, is something we can't afford to miss today. They neglected to talk to us about money and money decisions.

Money can't be taboo any longer. We have to stop trying to compete, and start trying to help each other. It all starts in the family home. I will talk money with anyone outside of our home that wants to, but I don't push people to do it. I hope that someday our kids will live in a society that embraces these conversations more.

Once we understand the differences in how men and women view money, it is easy to see why so many marriages buckle under the pressure of financial stress. Men view money as a source of ego, and women view money as a source of security.

Men, if you want to sit down with your wife and talk about your budget, do not start the conversation with "if we don't stop spending we are going to default on our mortgage." While this is a perfectly logical statement in your mind, it ignites a sense of fear in your wife that you cannot even comprehend. She thinks you have just blamed her for spending too much, and that you are going to lose your home.

Women, if you want to get your husband's attention and talk about your budget, do not start the conversation with "I don't even know how we ended up in this mess; we aren't making enough money to make ends meet." While this is perfectly logical in your mind, you have just hit a man where it hurts him the most. His ego. You have all but accused him of being incompetent in managing the household finances, and insinuated that he does not have a job that is sufficient for your family's needs.

Neither of these statements is going to create a healthy, productive, open conversation around money. Instead, we need to approach our finance discussions based on feelings and values.

Perhaps you feel like you are so in control of your finances, that this doesn't apply to you. On the other hand, perhaps you make so much money, that the day-to-day burden of personal finance doesn't have to be talked about in your household. Alternatively, perhaps you are so busy, that you don't have, or want to, take time out of your day to talk about your finances.

Regardless of where your relationship with money is at today, you need to talk with your spouse about it for the sake of your kids. By sitting down and talking about what really matters in your life, you will be able to model a different set of behaviors for your children. They are watching everything you do, and everything you say. Teach them with a level of intention! If you want them to be more, you need to model more.

Creating your financial and family values does not have to be a hard task. It doesn't have to be a long drawn out conversation. But if you want your kids to be financially educated, it needs to happen.

If you are the person who manages the budget, let your spouse know that you love them and that you want both of you to be involved in understanding your finances. Tell them that you value their input, and that you think you could do better if everyone had a say.

If you don't have a budget, tell your spouse that you think it is something that might help. Tell them that you see possibilities for more, and that it might be nice to look at your finances on paper.

When you have that first money conversation, create some ground rules. Either of you can talk about behaviours, only if it is about your own behaviours. Talk about how YOUR behaviours are affecting the budget. Talk about how YOUR behaviors are making you feel. If you are buying things without asking your spouse, tell them. Be open and honest, and be genuine. Tell them that you believe you can do better together, and you need their help. Most importantly, talk from a place of love and a desire to do better.

When I finally opened the door on our finances to my wife, I felt an overwhelming sense of relief. I no longer had to be the expert. I didn't have to bear the burden and stress that I had been holding onto for so long. I was finally able to listen from a place of learning, and through learning, I was finally able to communicate.

In the few conversations we had in the past, she had recommended switching to cash instead of credit. Each time I told her that we didn't need to. She asked how much we had available to spend each month after our bills, and I struggled to give her a number. I remember thinking to myself "the budget is complex; it can't be broken down into a simple number." Then I convinced myself that I had all the burden, because I had all the knowledge.

With a little financial literacy, my wife was able to show me how to frame our budget in a way that communicated to her. My complex financial model was OK for another accountant, but it didn't work for most people. Heck, it didn't even work for me!

Once I simplified the budget file, I quickly saw the number she so desperately wanted. Moreover, I quickly agreed to switch to cash. She was instrumental in the format of the budget template you see today.

Finally, we were able to talk about our money in a way that was healthy. I told her that I was stressed about making enough money to fund the lifestyle we had become accustomed to. I told her that I needed her help. From there, things really started to change for us.

We sat down to figure out what really mattered. We went through each line in our budget and asked ourselves if that line matched with the things we wanted for our life. For the things we wanted in our kids' lives. We made an agreement on how we would look at our money, how we would model our financial values, and how we would create a new landscape for our kids. We were going to be intentional about how we interacted with money, and how we wanted our kids to interact with money in their life.

Once my wife and I were on the same page, we started communicating with our kids about money as well. When we are presented with choices that involve everyone, we involve everyone in making that choice. To our surprise, this is another area that has saved us a significant amount of money over the course of a year.

For example, in the past when presented with a day of excursions, my wife and I would decide what we thought the kids would enjoy and then tell them where we were going. We always picked places that had an entrance fee and cost money to see, because we wanted our kids to experience something new. As parents, we knew what they would like.

Much to our surprise, when we started presenting our kids with several options to choose from, they often choose the cheapest one. Our kids choose the option that gives them the most time with us. They choose the options that they know they will love.

*"Your kids will remember your presence, not your presents."*

The first step on your path to better, is your budget. Take the time to get it right, so that we can move up the family finance levels we talk about next.

## CHAPTER 9

# THE THREE LEVELS OF FAMILY FINANCE

If you want to get out of debt fast, and live off rice and beans, you can. Some of you reading this book likely need to. However, if you are looking to provide something incrementally better for your family and live a financially healthier life, spend the time to put the values we talked about in place, before applying anything else. They will put you in a position to work together as a team, and make decisions that help your entire family be better.

If you have adopted some of the values we talked about (hopefully all of them), you should now have a budget in place, and you should know whether you are living within your means.

Excluding those families that are already in crisis, most families fall into three financial levels. The first level refers to those families that are looking to find some financial stability in their lives. This situation arises when you are living beyond your current level of income, and can show up in many forms. Regardless of how it shows up, it is usually the result of negative monthly cash flow, or spending beyond your means.

The second situation level refers to those families that have some level of financial stability, but are now looking for ways to improve. They are trying to see if they can use some of their financial discipline to reduce debt, and/or increase investments. Sometimes, they are looking to see if they can live off less, in order to work less and spend more time with family. When you are in the second level, you are trying to figure out how to lower the cost of your life, so that you can lower the amount of income you need to fund it, over the long-term. You are now in the beginning phases of modelling the *Your Life, Your Income* methodology.

Once families have risen out of the second level, they find themselves in the growth and accumulation phase. Alternatively, in the new era, perhaps they are looking solely for freedom from working on someone else's terms, and trying to figure out how to exit the time trade. You are trying to pay down your house, increase your investments, and accumulate wealth.

Regardless of which level you currently find yourself in, all three levels require you to have financial values in place, and a desire to model something better, for the future, and for your kids. You have made a choice to take back control of your finances, so that banks, work, and society, no longer control you. You are ready to implement simple strategies that allow you to do more with your money.

Let us review each of these levels to help you determine where you and your family currently sit.

## LEVEL 1 – FINANCIAL STABILITY

Financial stability is hard for any family that finds themselves in a negative cash flow position. You have likely found yourself in a position where you just keep falling further and further behind. You struggle to make all of your payments each month, and are constantly accessing your line of credit or meeting with the bank to consolidate debt. If you are, as we were, you hold multiple forms of debt. This debt includes your house, one or two cars, a personal loan or line of credit, and you have balances on at least one or more credit cards. Just when you get one thing paid off, it seems like you have run a new balance up on something else. You are making minimum payments on everything you have, and just when you feel like you are making some progress, you have to come up with more money to spend on something new for your kids.

You, and the another sixty percent of parents, are in fact living paycheck to paycheck. If you have any money saved for retirement, it is not much, and you have nothing set aside for emergencies. You hear that you should have investments in place for your kids' education, and feel guilty that you haven't put more away. You are struggling to keep your head above water and it is stressing you out. You continue to work harder, only to find the same things happen repeatedly.

With many of the families that find themselves looking for financial stability, they have created budgets in the past, but they are not up to date. It seems like a useless exercise, because whatever you create becomes meaningless within days, or weeks of a review. Most couples haven't updated their budget in several months, and many don't know exactly what their income level is. They only know that it is not enough to fund the life they want.

You are not alone. I was in this exact same spot and facing a fifty percent cut in pay. Once we put some financial values in place, opened up the lines of communication in our home, and created a passion for eliminating our reliance on debt, we found ourselves quickly on a path toward stability.

## LEVEL 2 – FINANCIAL IMPROVEMENT

Now that you have created a stable financial environment in your home, you will feel a little relief from the stress that has been building. You will have moments where you are excited about what you have accomplished, and feel passionate about making more changes. Unfortunately, you will have other moments that still cause you anxiety. Surprisingly, as you and your spouse try to make the transition into improving your finances, you will face more decisions than you did when creating stability. In level one, spending decisions were easy, because the focus was on cutting, not on spending. You both knew that in order to get your head out of the water, you had to work together to stop overconsumption, and you had to work together to reduce your committed costs. In level two, it becomes more about your goals, and creating positive momentum that your family benefits from.

We found that setting small goals, and rewarding ourselves often, were extremely important as we started our journey of improvement. We needed to celebrate our wins, and be 100% committed to the open lines of communication we had created. When one person had an inkling to spend on a want, the other had to step in and talk reason. We had to continue to function as a well-oiled machine.

When you are in level two, you will still feel like it is a challenge to get ahead. Don't worry, with a little momentum, you will quickly see a change in perspective. Your relationship

CHAPTER 9 - THE THREE LEVELS OF FAMILY FINANCE

with your spouse, and your relationship with your kids will start to improve, and that will be a key benefit that you should recognize.

Once you are in the improvement stage, you will have eliminated several of your debts, and will likely have just your mortgage and a car loan remaining. You won't need to access your line of credit, because you will have an emergency fund set aside, and you won't be meeting with the bank, because you now see them for what they really are. You will only have one credit card (maximum) that you use for specific agreed upon items, like gas or booking travel, and you will have the discipline to pay it off before your next pay each month. You are now working the debt snowball and making progress on your remaining debt, and you have some investments in place for retirement, or your kids' education.

You are still living paycheck to paycheck, but only because you are making all of your income go to work. You have a working budget and review it at least once a month with your family. One portion of your income is going to committed costs, and the other is available as cash. Any balance of cash goes directly into your debt snowball, or an investment account.

Finally, you are making more of your kids' important events, and have re-aligned your personal and financial values.

## LEVEL 3 – FINANCIAL GROWTH AND ACCUMULATION

Congratulations! You have now moved up a level in your life. Not because you have purchased your way there, or because you have bunch of nice cars; instead, because you are living your life on your terms, and are free from the pressure of banks and Facebook newsfeeds. You are ready to pursue what you want, when you want it. You can accumulate wealth, free your time, and grow as a person. More importantly, you can grow exponentially as a parent.

Now that you have improved your financial landscape, you feel free for the first time in your life. You are excited about what you have accomplished, and feel passionate about helping others. Money is no longer a source of anxiety, and your decisions centre on what is best for *your* future. What is best for your family's future!

You aren't focused on cutting spending, because you understand that the secret to wealth and happiness is not based on how much you spend. You have discipline with your money, your focus is on experiences instead of things, and you use cash to fund your life. Your goals of today were your dreams of yesterday, and you are living the life you want for yourself. Congratulations!

When you are in level three, you are no longer struggling to get ahead. Your only struggle is how you will allocate your money, and how you will separate your income from your time. You aren't focused on improving your relationships with the people in your life, because your life is now about enjoying your time with them.

In level three, you will have eliminated all forms of debt, and be mortgage free, or applying all previous debt payments to your mortgage as the final step of the debt snowball. In less than seven years, you will have no debt at all, and a significant amount saved up for retirement. You have a large emergency fund built up, and you aren't worried about your credit rating, because you don't

CHAPTER 9 - THE THREE LEVELS OF FAMILY FINANCE

rely on credit anymore. You aren't living paycheck to paycheck, and each month you are reviewing your excess funds to allocate them out among all of your different investment vehicles. You are living the *Your Income, Your Life* dream.

I created a checklist so you can see quickly where you fall in each of the three levels. Before we go into the steps, you need to look at each level in order figure out where you sit today. Once you know where you are at, you can plan your path for progressing up each step of the ladder. You can download this checklist at *www.YourIncomeYourLife/checklist*.

| Looking for Financial Stability? | Ready for Financial Improvement? | Building Wealth and Freedom? |
|---|---|---|
| ☐ Have a budget, but it isn't up to date | ☐ Have a budget, and review it monthly | ☐ Do not carry credit card debt |
| ☐ Struggle communicating about finances | ☐ Communicating about finances regularly | ☐ Communicating about finances is fun |
| ☐ Living paycheck to paycheck | ☐ Living paycheck to paycheck | ☐ No longer living paycheck to paycheck |
| ☐ Negative cash flow | ☐ Balanced cash flow | ☐ Positive cash flow |
| ☐ Use credit card for all expenses | ☐ Do not carry credit card debt | ☐ Do not carry credit card debt |
| ☐ Personal loan debt | ☐ No personal loans | ☐ No personal loans |
| ☐ Balance on your line of credit | ☐ Line of credit eliminated | ☐ No line of credit |
| ☐ One or more car loans | ☐ Plan to attack your car loans | ☐ Eliminated all of your loans |
| ☐ Mortgage with more than 15 years left | ☐ Mortgage with more than 15 years left | ☐ Mortgage with less than 15 years left |
| ☐ No emergency fund available | ☐ Have a small emergency fund available | ☐ Have a substantial rainy day fund available |
| ☐ Little if anything saved for retirement | ☐ Have some money saved for retirement | ☐ Have accumulated some money for retirement |
| ☐ Little if anything saved for kids education | ☐ Have a little saved for kids education | ☐ Have accumulated some money for kids education |
| ☐ Struggling just to keep up | ☐ Struggling just to get ahead | ☐ Excited about personal and financial growth |
| ☐ Do not have a will or suitable life insurance | ☐ Have a will, but do not have suitable life insurance | ☐ Have a will and life insurance |

Now that you understand what level you are at, let us go into more detail on the levels of debt we live with.

# CHAPTER 10

# HOW MUCH DEBT IS TOO MUCH?

Do you know if your mortgage is putting a strain on the rest of your budget? Do you know if your cars are causing you to live paycheck to paycheck? Is your budget under stress because of your credit and debit cards? Is debt consolidation your only option, and does it make sense to refinance your house?

If you are financially literate, you should already know the answers to these questions. Nevertheless, just because you make more than the average household and you have more financial instruments to manage, doesn't necessarily mean you are financially knowledgeable.

Let us explore each of the five questions on debt, in relation to your financial stability.

## QUESTION#1 – ARE WE HOUSE POOR?

Banks used to approve mortgages that had total house payments up to 45% of your annual pre-tax income. This includes your mortgage payment, property taxes, and insurance. In the

## CHAPTER 10 - HOW MUCH DEBT IS TOO MUCH?

post-crisis lending world, mortgage lenders will still lend up to 35 percent of your pre-tax income, but I still would not classify this as financially healthy for the borrower.

On the flipside, debt extremists would advise that you should never tie up more than 25 percent of your take-home income (not pre-tax income) in your house. The key point is that you don't want to put a strain on the rest of your life, by tying up too much in your house. If you do, it will always be a struggle to pay cash for the things you need to buy, it will be a struggle to support the activities your kids want to participate in, and it will be a struggle to save up for retirement.

My recommendation is that your mortgage payments, excluding property taxes and insurance, should never exceed 25% of your annual <u>pre-tax</u> income. If we were to use the numbers from Exhibit 1, this would mean that someone with a monthly mortgage payment of $1,624 would have annual payments of $19,488. At the twenty-five percent threshold, they should have at least $77,952 in annual income (at a minimum) to ensure that they are not feeling house poor. Will this level make you feel strained? It likely will, but you can still do the things you want to do, to live your life in the same way you have grown accustomed. Will you be able to make a significant dent in your outstanding loans, or start putting more away money for retirement? Probably not.

To be financially healthy, I would much rather see someone in a 15-year term instead of the 20-year term, in which his or her annual payment would be $24,020 and require a minimum annual income of $96,080.

Does this one-size fit all approach work? Not all the time. Those living in Toronto, Vancouver, New York, San Francisco, or for example Sydney, will need to spend a much larger amount than that, just to live in a shoebox. In these instances, location, transportation, and other trade-offs are necessary to evaluate a healthy mortgage amount, before making a recommendation.

Perhaps you could avoid purchasing cars and use public transportation instead, saving a substantial amount of money annually on gas, insurance, parking, and maintenance. When you need to go out of town on weekends, rental cars are a viable option. My recommendation would be to rent at a lower monthly amount until you can save up enough of a down payment, so that when you do finally buy a home, your mortgage payments aren't going to strain your life.

## QUESTION #2 – DO WE OWN MORE CAR THAN OUR BUDGET CAN HANDLE?

Your principal residence and your mortgage are still considered one of the few forms of "good debt" on the market today. The rationale is good debt is associated with anything that does not depreciate in value. Cars on the other hand, depreciate. Moreover, they depreciate rapidly. I have purchased many new cars in my life, and I now look back and regret every one. I justified the excess purchase price by convincing myself that the new car warranty and the peace of mind was worth the premium I paid to own it.

Perhaps it was the new car smell, the fact that no one had ever driven it, or the ease in which I obtained financing. It certainly wasn't because we wanted a car that other kids hadn't gotten dirty. Right?

The quality of cars has changed drastically over the past 20 years. CAA reports that it costs on average $3,656 to run a mid-size car each year. This does not include maintenance, financing, or depreciation.

The moment you drive a new car of the lot, your car has lost approximately 15% of its original value, and another 10% of value over the balance of the first year. Each year thereafter, it will continue to decline at a rate of about 20%. Yes, cars depreciate rapidly.

If we had purchased two brand new cars at a cost of $50,000 (as in Exhibit 1), they would only be worth $38,250 after one year of driving. Unfortunately, that means our loan would be upside down after just 12 months, given that we only paid $9,660 over that same period (leaving a balance on the loan of at least $40,340, assuming zero percent financing).

This means that we paid a premium of over $2,000 in the first year alone.

OK Jeff, you haven't figured in the cost of maintenance on a used car, so that isn't a fair analysis. Sure, just as I did for many years, you can try to justify the cost of owning a new car based on the savings on potential repairs. However, how many times have you had a significant repair in the last 10 years? I bet you can count those examples up on one hand.

According to DesRosiers Automotive Consultants, in year five, the annual repair cost of a vehicle is only $800 (on average), and by year seven, it rises to between $1,000 and $1,100 annually.

So let us examine the impact of buying a new car vs a used car, over the course of five years.

*Exhibit 2*

| Brand New Car | | | | | | Used Car - 5 years old | | | | | |
|---|---|---|---|---|---|---|---|---|---|---|---|
| Purchase price | $ | 20,000 | | | | Purchase price | $ | 6,300 | | | |
| | | Deprec | | Maint | Total | | | Deprec | | Maint | Total |
| Year 1 | $ | 4,700 | $ | 300 | $ 5,000 | Year 1 | $ | 1,481 | $ | 800 | $ 2,281 |
| Year 2 | $ | 3,060 | $ | 345 | $ 3,405 | Year 2 | $ | 964 | $ | 900 | $ 1,864 |
| Year 3 | $ | 2,448 | $ | 397 | $ 2,845 | Year 3 | $ | 771 | $ | 1,000 | $ 1,771 |
| Year 4 | $ | 1,958 | $ | 476 | $ 2,435 | Year 4 | $ | 617 | $ | 1,100 | $ 1,717 |
| Year 5 | $ | 1,567 | $ | 800 | $ 2,367 | Year 5 | $ | 494 | $ | 1,155 | $ 1,649 |
| Total | $ | 13,733 | $ | 2,318 | $ 16,051 | Total | $ | 4,326 | $ | 4,955 | $ 9,281 |

After five years, you can see that we would have paid a premium of $6,770 to buy the car brand new, excluding financing costs.

Why is it that, we continue to buy into the notion that buying new and financing, is the better option?[9]

If you want to live a financially healthy life, you may want to consider buying used cars and keeping the total value of all purchases below 25% of your annual income. Better yet, save up and pay cash for that next vehicle, even if it means you are driving something more than 5 years old.

## QUESTION #3 – ARE CREDIT CARDS EVIL?

"Tear up your credit cards, you don't need them."

We have all heard this advice from the financial gurus out there. Will you tear them up? Likely not.

In the modern era of purchasing, many retail workers frown on cash payments. So few customers do it, and many times, it is hard to make adequate change. We have online purchases, hotel rooms, plane tickets, and reward programs to consider.

---

[9] http://www.theglobeandmail.com/globe-drive/news/the-real-cost-of-car-ownership/article1378882/

## CHAPTER 10 - HOW MUCH DEBT IS TOO MUCH?

So, how do we create a healthy relationship with money in this technologically advanced age?

If possible, I would encourage you to avoid using credit cards for clothes, groceries, and entertainment. When you are physically shopping, always use cash when possible. We need to understand, that consumers spend on average, 12-18% more when shopping with credit (or debit), then they do when using cash.

Retailers know this, and that is why they are willing to pay banks and credit card companies a fee for accepting them. The fee of 3-4% is substantially lower than the incremental sales they see when accepting these forms of payment.

I still hold a credit card today. The difference however, is in the way in which we use them. We only have one, and my wife and I talk about any purchase we are going to make with that card, before we make it.

We use it for hotels, airlines, and for online purchases, because we agree that it makes sense for us. I should also note that we pay our cards off prior to our next paycheck, and both our cards (debit and credit) are on cash back programs, which we take advantage of every Christmas.

In general, the reason we talk about each purchase before making it, results from the nature of the purchases we are making. They are discretionary purchases. All of our needs can be purchased using cash, in all situations. As such, we do just that.

By agreeing to talk about credit or debit card purchases, we are making decisions together on how we spend our discretionary money. We also use these discussions to verify that we have the money in our accounts, thereby ensuring we don't spend money we don't have.

Why do we pay them off before our next paycheck?

Because it creates a discipline of spending within our means. We aren't borrowing from next month to pay for something we want this month. If we are going to buy it, we want it to come from our positive monthly cash flow.

If you are going to make a conscious decision to have a credit card, I strongly urge you to operate with one card, talk about your expenses each time, and pay it off each month, prior to your next income installment.

If you decide to keep a credit card, here are my recommendations for how to use them in a healthy manner:

- Always pay it off
- Always budget for the things you will charge to it
- Don't use it for emergencies (use cash or another form of credit if absolutely necessary)
- Agree with your spouse on the items you will, and will not, use it for
- Always have a cashback reward program on your card

## QUESTION #4 – SHOULD WE CONSOLIDATE OUR LOANS?

The process of repaying loans can be stressful. The stress of working multiple payments into a budget is a daunting task for parents that are experiencing new expenses for the first time. There is also the issue of different interest rates for each loan, different payment dates, and different lenders.

Having to repay multiple institutions over multiple payment dates, does increase your likelihood of missing a payment, and likely your overall interest costs. As a result, defaulting on your

## CHAPTER 10 - HOW MUCH DEBT IS TOO MUCH?

loans, centralizing your payments through one institution, and lowering your interest costs are all enticing reasons as to why you may be considering consolidating your debt.

It's a great idea in theory.

You can reduce the amount you owe each month to make your payments more manageable by going with one amortization period over a slightly longer period.

Not only that, you may be able to lock in at an interest rate for the one new loan that's lower than the rates your current loans carry.

But does that benefit outweigh the risk, and does consolidation create a healthier financial situation for you and your family? Likely not. In addition, we haven't addressed the issue that caused us to get into multiple forms of debt in the first place.

Over-consumption, spending beyond our means, and a lack of discipline, have caused us to borrow from tomorrow what we can't afford today. The society we live in, and the banks we use, have convinced us that not only can we afford more, we deserve more. We tell ourselves, that reducing spending will affect our kids' lives, and we continue to make the same mistakes we always have.

In reality, the only one that wins in a consolidation is the bank that you consolidate with. They convince you that one loan over 5 years at 3%, is better than three loans over multiple periods (let's say all three add up to 3 years) at 5%. I would argue differently, and here is why:

The bank will combine your three loans into one and convince you that you are saving money because they are giving you an interest rate that is 2% better than what you are currently getting. Not only that, they will show you that total monthly payment is lower under the consolidation loan that what you were paying when you added the other three together. They are correct, you are paying less each month, but now you are making payments over a longer period. If you had three $3000 loans and consolidated them into one $9000 loan, you would now pay a total of $1,173 in interest. If you didn't consolidate, and paid off those loans over three years, you would have only paid $710 in interest.

More than likely, those three loans would have also had staggered maturity dates, and if you applied the minimum payment from the first one paid off to the second, you would lower your interest costs further.

Instead of consolidation, consider increasing payments on your lowest value loan. Once you get the positive feedback of paying it off, roll the minimum payment amount into the second loan and watch it disappear as well. You will start to get some immediate feedback about the changes you are making in your spending behaviours, and momentum will fuel the fire. Dave Ramsey refers to this as the debt snowball, and it works![10]

The general rule of thumb is to increase your payments if you want to improve your financial landscape; don't decrease them. When you decrease them, you will only suffer by paying the banks more, and feeling stressed about your money over a longer period. I would never recommend consolidation loans if you can avoid it. However, if you must, make the decision to radically change your values, and live the concepts in this book, so you never have to do it again.

---

10   http://www.daveramsey.com/blog/get-out-of-debt-with-the-debt-snowball-plan/

## QUESTION #5 – SHOULD WE REFINANCE OUR HOUSE?

I have heard this question numerous times. We hear about new products, and start to believe that refinancing is the best solution for our family. The question comes in many forms, such as:

- Should I open up a home-equity line of credit?
- Should I refinance to get a better interest rate?
- Should I consolidate all of my debt and collapse it into my mortgage?
- Should I switch to a floating line of credit on my home in lieu of a mortgage?
- Should I refinance to get a shorter amortization period?

Please don't be fooled, these are all re-financing scenarios.

Other than refinancing to get a better interest rate, each scenario is increasing your potential debt liability. Is that a financially healthy decision? Usually, the answer is no. It all depends on the reason you are refinancing in the first place.

This is another situation in which a one-size answer does not suit all situations. As a general rule of thumb, if you are refinancing to get a lower interest rate, and the fees are paid back from the interest savings in less than 2 years, AND you have more than 8 years left on your mortgage, refinancing is a healthy decision. If you are refinancing to help your family avoid a financial crisis, it can be a healthy decision, so long as you address the underlying issues that caused the crisis in the first place. I would very rarely recommend this as an option to consider.

You should now understand acceptable levels of debt in relation to the income you make, and should be able to make educated decisions on how your debt will be managed in the context of your family budget. Now it is time to create some financial stability in our lives.

# CHAPTER 11

# BUDGETING FOR STABILITY

In our situation, we didn't realize we lacked financial stability because we made enough money to create it every three or four months. Each time a large bonus check came in, we had a glimpse of what financial stability was, only to revert back to our destructive behaviours of over-consumption in the days that followed. We would rack up our debt, and worry about paying it off the next time a check came in.

Thank goodness, we saw that these behaviours were going to destroy us, before they actually did.

When my wife and I finally sought out financial stability, we found ourselves in a discussion around our personal values, and what mattered most in our life. For the first time, we were about to start prioritizing the things we were spending money on, and creating alignment between what we valued, and our expenditures.

We needed to find adjustments so that we could lower the cost of our lives, without lowering the standard in which we wanted to raise our family. We talked about our house and our cars. We talked about the landscaping services, and our housekeeper. We talked about what we were paying for cable and Internet, and we talked about the kids' activities. We talked about everything, and we did so without judgement.

Whatever your situation, your budget will open up the lines of communication. If you create an environment free of judgement, and work toward the values we discussed earlier, I am confident this discussion will bring you closer together. It did for us.

Financial stability happens when you take back control over your money. It occurs once you are no longer spending more money than you are going to make. When you are financially stable, you are following a working budget, and have cut enough of your monthly expenses, so that you are living within your means. You have a will in place to protect your assets and provide for your family's future in case something should happen to you. In addition you have an emergency fund set aside, so that you don't blow your budget each time something unexpected in life comes up.

Let's explore the components of your budget in order to realize where you have the opportunities to cut some of your expenses, without sacrificing your quality of life.

## IF YOU WANT TO BUILD A FUTURE, YOU MUST CLEAN UP THE PAST

How do we know where we should cut? What expenses can we change? These were the questions that ran through our heads. These are the first part of your committed costs that you should be reviewing. We talked about these in the previous chapter.

## CHAPTER 11 - BUDGETING FOR STABILITY

If you want to transition from financial stability, to financial improvement, you need to get your debt back in line with acceptable standards. It is your life, so you decide. In our case, we weren't house poor, but our mortgage was right on the high end of the range. We really like our home and all the things we have done to it. We have moved enough over the past five years, and want our kids to settle into an area and have a school they like. Moving just wasn't an option we were willing to consider, so we knew that we would have to look elsewhere in our budget as a result.

We examined our key expenses, however, the one area that my wife and I had overlooked for too long, was how much we were spending on our cars. While I was not working, we actually had our Murano sitting in the garage for months at a time, and we were still making payments on it. When we finally realized how stupid that was, we had a difficult time finding someone to buy it.

We sat down and explored every possible option. We finally settled on the fact that we could trade in the Murano and eliminate some additional debt. The car my wife loved, was upside down in relation to our loan, and was replaced by a very small, economical vehicle, that would get me to and from work. I mention this to highlight you should not overlook anything. Review every loan you have in your budget, and figure out what is really affecting the quality of your life. Then, decide together what you are going to cut.

## PURGING INSTEAD OF SPLURGING

There is another option when it comes to paying down some of your debt and reducing your commitments. I spent years splurging on all the things I thought would bring me happiness in those moments, only to find out they were piling up in the basement. Whether it is excess furniture, cars, boats, or other items you've accumulated over the years, it is time to see if they are worth keeping in light of your current situation. I call it purging.

We had moved several times in the short span of five years, and we finally decided it was time to clean out our backroom in the basement. After realizing all the items we had, we decided to purge in order get out of the debt we had just incurred. We cleaned out our basement, and held a garage sale two weeks later. We sold the bigger items on Kijiji, and at the end of this exercise, we had come up with an astonishing $2850. We had almost three thousand dollars worth of "things" in our basement that we hadn't used in years.

Look at the list of debt you created, and figure out what you could sell to make up enough money to eliminate the lowest value loan you have. You will instantly increase your cash flow, without losing anything that will affect your quality of life. The bigger the item, the bigger the cash flow impact!

## CUT YOUR REMAINING COMMITMENTS

Now that you see the impact your debt has on your life, and you realize that you are spending more than the money you have available each month, you have an appreciation for why your debt has been escalating. It makes sense that you have been struggling to keep up.

It is time to review all of your other committed costs. Sit down and review, in detail, each monthly contract or bill you have. There are tons of money saving ideas if you spend the time understanding what you are actually paying for.

Have you looked at your property tax assessment? Is the assessed value accurate? Did you know that you can challenge it? This is one area that we often overlook. If your home is not assessed at the correct value, in most cities, there is an appeals process you can follow.

What are the deductibles on your house insurance policy? Is your replacement value correct? Does it exclude the cost of your land? Are you paying for things you might not really need coverage for? Go through your insurance bill in detail, starting with the biggest premium amounts and working your way down.

Are you using more than you have to for your hydro, gas, or water? Can you change the times in which you do laundry, or turn the air conditioning up a few degrees? Better yet, can you turn it off altogether? Do you have a clothesline you can hang your clothes on from time to time. There are lots of ways to reduce your consumption as it relates to energy. Not only will it help your budget, it will help the environment at the same time. Hop online and check out some of the green websites to find lots of ideas on reducing energy consumption in the home. Look online for carbon footprint calculators, and search for green initiatives in the home.

Are you really watching all of the TV channels you are paying for? Could you get away with basic cable or better yet, no cable at all? Does everyone need the cell phone plan they have today, or can you get rid of your home phone all together? We were able to cut our bill by $150 without noticing any changes to the things we did with our phones, or our TV.

Can you cancel the magazine subscriptions you have, or read the paper online? Can you exercise using your body weight and find other activities to keep fit? Do you really need that cleaning service or landscaping company? Everything should be on the table for review.

Go through each line item and figure out what is really important to how you want to live your lives, and remember, your kids value your time more than anything else!

## SAVE WITH CASH

What we found is by creating values that governed our behaviour towards money, we were naturally setup to improve our financial stability. When you use cash for everything that is not committed, you can only use what you have. It facilitates the discipline you are trying to create with your budget, and gives you a visual aid that is tangible. It is something you can see, feel, and associate with. As it depletes, you get immediate feedback on how you are doing. You can make conscious choices about spending and I guarantee you will see an immediate improvement in how you manage your money. Let's be honest, while you aren't in a crisis, if you are looking for stability you were on a path to crisis, and need to make some significant changes in your life. Cash is still king, whether society wishes to admit it or not.

When my wife first talked to me about switching to cash, I felt an overwhelming feeling of anxiety. Fear creeped into my soul, and I started to come up with multiple reasons on why this made no sense. However, deep down I knew she was right. I knew what she was telling me, and I knew that we needed to make this change if we wanted any chance at making our budget work.

## CHAPTER 11 - BUDGETING FOR STABILITY

That decision was one of the most important decisions we made together. I like to say we made it together, but let's be honest, she made it, and it just took me a long time to admit she was right.

After we had cleaned up our budget, we could clearly see how much we had available to spend on things that weren't already committed. That was our cash amount, and it was impossible to stick to, when using credit. With credit cards, we couldn't see the how much we had left at any given time, and we couldn't feel how our purchases were impacting our budget. Each month, we would end up spending more than we planned.

I remember the first month when we switched to cash. I had to make a stop at Costco on the way home from work because we were out of paper towels and meat. I took $100 out of our drawer that morning, and figured that it was enough for the things we said we needed.

As I walked through the store, for the first time, I started seeing how retail stores get us as consumers. They put their highest margin, most attractive, unneeded items along the aisles that you have to walk through. These things are setup right in front of you as you walk in, and they show sale signs everyone. How can we live without them? It is such a steal! In the past, I may have been lured in, but not this time. This time was different. I knew I only had $100, and I had to get the things we needed as a family before anything else.

I picked up the meat we needed and started adding the numbers in my head. Wow, I was already at $78. I had less than $22 left to buy the paper towels and granola bars we also needed.

They had no paper towels, so as it turns out, I had just enough money to buy the large box of granola bars. I was out of cash, and instead of walking back through the store, or throwing other items in the cart, I went to the checkout, and paid my $99 bill.

Using cash probably saved me $100 in my very first shopping experience with it. Beaming with pride, I went home and told my wife how successful I had been while shopping. Then, my excitement got the best of me and I said:

"Let's cut-up our credit cards!"

We didn't. Thank God my wife is much more rational than I am. We have found that credit cards do work for certain transactions, but without a doubt, in the majority of situations cash works best. Why? Because it forces us to make a conscious decision about spending our money, at the time we are spending it. For starters, you can't spend more than what you have. We bring what we think we need for each excursion we go on. Gone are the days of spending $300 on groceries. We realized how painful it was to hand over $300 to a cashier and started couponing. Gone are the days of spending $100 to go out for dinner as a family. We realized how much extra food we were ordering, once we had to fork over our hard-earned cash at the end of the meal. And gone are the days of making big dollar purchases on impulse, because we don't have the cash on hand to make them.

Take away the ability to act on impulse, and you will stop acting on impulse. It is actually pretty simple.

We were getting 1-4% back on all purchases made with our debit or credit cards, and we were getting back $1,200 each year. That means we had charged at least $30,000 to our credit card over the course of 12 months (assuming we got 4% back on every purchase, which isn't a reality). If we were overspending by 10% each time, that meant we were spending $3,000 per year more than we planned.

I know we are saving a lot more, because we have cut out over $9,000 from our expenses in the past year, and I attribute most of it to our discipline using cash. Our goal is to use cash for all of our major purchases going forward, and do everything in our power, to avoid going into any new form of debt, ever again. So far, this goal is motivating us, and yielding the results we want.

## MANAGING RISK

There are two things that we shouldn't overlook when examining your financial stability. As parents, you need to make sure that you have a will in place so everyone else knows what you want to happen with your money, your possessions, and your property, if you happen to die. You also need to make sure you have an emergency fund in place, so that you have a fighting chance when you are trying to manage to your budget each month.

**A legal will**—most parents understand how important a will is, the moment they find out they are expecting. If you are one of those people, this is one area that you can already check off, and move on. If not, you need to take action right away. Do not leave this up to local laws. They will not distribute it in the way that you intend to!

More than anything, it is vital to have a will if you have children or family that depend on you financially. Not only does it dictate who gets what, your will also decides who should look after your children if both parents go. Your will facilitates the proper financial arrangements for your kids as they grow up.

Designate that your finances go into a trust, and the legal guardians you have appointed can withdraw funds in order to provide the quality of life you want for your kids. In the trust, you can also decide how those funds will be invested, and you can decide on the rules that need to be followed for withdrawal. Perhaps you want to specify how your kids can use the money when they are 18, and ready for college, so that they don't come into a large sum all at once without the experience to manage it properly.

Getting a will does not cost a lot, and there are tons of local lawyers that you can go see. If you have waited this long, and are in a situation where you are trying to find financial stability, don't try to figure it out yourself. Just go get a professional to help.

**Emergency funds**—if you really want to live a healthy lifestyle and make your budget work month after month, you need to have a savings account with enough money in it to pay for the unexpected events in life. Whether it is to replace your vacuum cleaner, get rid of the skunk under your shed, a broken pipe in your basement bathroom, or a lawn infested by grubs, you will be able to react withoutderailing your budget (all of those things happened to us in the past month alone). Unexpected events happen that you can't budget for, especially with young kids, so you need to have some money set aside.

How much? At a minimum, you need to have at least $1,000 saved up. When you are in level 1, you don't have the benefit of positive cash flow to create a large rainy day fund. You need something in place so that you can see the result of your disciplined efforts, which will show up by balancing your budget each month. Agree with your spouse on the things that will qualify as an emergency, and only use these funds if you have to. A general rule of thumb is: a want is not an emergency, while a need is. However, it is your life, so you need to figure it out for your family's individual situation.

We will talk about increasing your emergency fund in the next chapter, where I like to refer to it as your rainy day fund.

## WHAT'S NEXT?

Once you have implemented the changes you worked as a team to identify, you need to start living within your budget. I suggest working in this fashion for at least three months so that you can model the discipline you need to work to a budget, and you can say with confidence that you are cash neutral. When you have, you are ready to move on to focus on improving your financial landscape.

# CHAPTER 12

# THE IMPROVEMENT PATH

Working budget–check.

Neutral cash flow–check.

Credit card debt gone–check.

Cash is king–check.

It is time to start attacking the rest of your debt aggressively, and shift from falling behind, to getting ahead.

Once we were most of our way through this process, we were able to get 75 percent of our debt paid off and significantly redefine our living expenses. We were in a position where our life was going to cost much less, and our income was no longer the driving force behind our consumption.

I left the job I felt trapped in, the job I had always wanted, and traded in the seventy-hour weeks for nine months at home with my family. Finally, I was going to be present. Present physically, and present in mind, because I didn't have work to consume me. It was the best nine months of my life!

I waited patiently until I found a job that matched my

personal values. That job pays fifty percent less than what I was making before. Is it worth it? Yes. I eat breakfast with my kids every morning, and I eat dinner with them every single night. When I am with them, I am thinking about them, and when I am at work, I can think about work. Who knew there was this other world out there? It is amazing.

I will outline six improvement steps you can take in order to create a healthier relationship with your money. However, before I do, we need to talk about how you communicate as a family.

## MONTHLY BUDGET MEETINGS

Ever since our first initial meeting, my wife and I agreed that we would have a budget meeting at least once per month. We have them immediately before our monthly pay is deposited. They were very hard a first, because it is hard to differentiate between needs and wants, especially when you have kids. We worry about what other kids will think if our daughters don't have any books to pick up at school through the book club orders. We worry about everything in the modern era when it comes to the best things for our children. We worry because we are human. We relate back to our own experiences and project them onto today. Once you acknowledge those worries, I can tell you, the meetings get easier. They get easier because of all the values you are implementing alongside the meetings. The differentiation between needs and wants becomes clearer when real cash changes hands, and when we involve our kids in the decisions that impact them. You will be surprised what you find out.

# CHAPTER 12 - THE IMPROVEMENT PATH

In our budgeting meeting, we cover three basic things:

1. We review the budget for the upcoming month to see how much cash is available after all of our committed costs.
2. Then we figure out how we will spend our cash items.
3. Finally, we make decisions on what we want to do with any cash left over from the month that just passed.

When we review our budget, we include our minimum debt payments in the committed costs section, and then see if we have any excess positive cash flow for the month coming.

After our committed costs, we can see how much cash is available for our "cash" spending. Our cash spending includes everything that is not automatically taken from our accounts, with the exception of gas for our vehicles. The goal is simple, end up the month with cash in hand.

If there is positive cash flow, we decide together on what we want to do with it. We might put an extra payment into our lowest debt, we might decide to treat ourselves to a nice dinner, or we might buy something that we have been putting off. We make the decision together, every single time, no matter the amount.

Finally, if we do really well and have more cash than expected at the end of the month, we make a decision on what we want to do with that. Put more money into our tax-free savings account? Pay down more debt? Or, keep it for next month's cash costs?

By meeting each month, we ensure that our budget works for us. If you want to improve financially you need to check in against your plan on a regular basis. By meeting monthly, we are able to dedicate the time we need, to stay on the same page.

CHAPTER 12 - THE IMPROVEMENT PATH

## WE TALK ABOUT WHAT WE NEED, BEFORE WE BUY IT

As parents, there are many financial decisions to make that don't impact the kids directly. For those things, we obviously aren't going to involve everyone in the house. However, if we want our kids to see money as a healthy topic, my wife and I have to feel comfortable talking about these things in front of them.

So many books out there preach about the things you need to teach your kids, but they forget to address the fact that modern-day finances are tough. As parents, we need to show our kids that we don't have all the answers, and that we are going to make mistakes with our money. We need to show our kids that we learn from our mistakes, and that mistakes make us stronger. We need to show our kids that our spending is not a secret, and that we make better decisions together.

Money helps us in every single aspect of our lives. We need money for shelter, food, clothes, transportation, activities, and school. We use money every day. That gives us an opportunity to talk about money every day. We embrace that opportunity.

My wife and I talk about what we need, before we buy it. This was a big adjustment for us, and took time to get used to. The feelings of anxiety and guilt started to pass, and our conversations became easier and easier. Our kids hear those conversations, and it forces us to have them in a constructive way. It helps our kids see that we can disagree and work through things, instead of getting angry or upset. In this way, it isn't only helping our kids learn about money, it is improving our marriage at the same time!

## WE REWARD OURSELVES FOR PROGRESS

We set goals as a family that help us improve our financial health. It may be to save up money to pay for a family vacation, or to make an extra payment on our mortgage. We are constantly striving to better our situation, and goals play an important part. With an end in mind, we find we are making progress each month.

Why are we able to make progress each time? Because we reward ourselves each time we achieve one of our goals. It is so important to take the time to celebrate your achievements, and creates yet another opportunity to talk to your kids about financial health. Whether that reward is taking a trip, going out for dinner, or simply spending a day at the beach, it really doesn't matter. Create goals for yourself which are achievable in a relatively short period. When the task doesn't seem so large, and there is a reward at the end of it, it is much easier to keep the momentum rolling!

## THE SIX STEPS

Here are the 6 steps you need to take when improving your financial landscape:

*Step 1 – Get the correct life insurance in place*

*Step 2 – Start your debt snowball*

*Step 3 – Build a rainy day fund*

*Step 4 – Look for ways to increase income*

*Step 5 – Re-instate your company match*

*Step 6 – Setup your kid's education funds*

You may recognize a few of these steps from the Dave Ramsey baby steps. If you are in a similar position to what we are, you have already completed some of these steps, but not in the order Dave laid out. We had money sitting in investment accounts, money in our retirement accounts, and some money saved for our kids' education. However, we didn't have a clear plan of attack for the our debt. We had no idea on how we were going to start getting ahead, especially considering our income was going to drop.

So where do we start?

Do we take money out of our retirement savings and pay off debt? Do we take money from our investment accounts and put it into a savings account for emergencies? Do we stop investing in our company pension plans, or our kids tax sheltered education funds?

We decided the answer to these questions was no.

We were going to live the same life we had grown accustomed to living, but lower the costs that it was taking to do it. We were going to work the baby steps starting at step 2, as if we had no choice but to start there.

Before we did that however, we needed to get the right life insurance in place.

## STEP 1 – LIFE INSURANCE

Life insurance is one of those complex financial instruments I talked about in Chapter 2. Financial institutions have created products based on the fears people have, not necessarily, because the product helps us.

The only form of insurance you need is a term life insurance policy. Likely, for a period lasting five years more than when your mortgage will be paid in full. Why? Because you are now going to be focusing on your financial health. If you create discipline and roll the payment from your first loan into your second, and your second into your third, you will be debt-free in less than five years. Do that with your mortgage, and you can be debt free in ten years. Increase your income sources, and you can do it much faster.

Let us say your mortgage has twenty years left on it today. That means you will have ten years where you can accumulate retirement savings or wealth. Moreover, in the event of your death, those investments will be available to fund your life. You only need life insurance to get you to the point in which you will be able to live off the passive income from what you have saved up. Likely in about twenty years! Moreover, if you don't have kids, you need a lot less in insurance, because you don't have anyone that relies on your income.

In order to have your insurance policy fund your family's expenses, the general rule of thumb is to have at least ten times your annual income. Assuming you direct those funds to be in an established growth fund that shows 10% return, your policy will passively fund your family's life. You will in essence, be self-insured.

Unfortunately, the majority of life insurance policies held today are cash value insurance policies, or universal policies. Both put you in a position to overpay. They are great for the insurance company, but terrible for us as consumers. I know, because I have held both. Held as in past tense.

Let me explain.

**Cash Value**—These policies provide two different streams. You have your life insurance portion, which is relatively low, but grows as you age. The other portion is a cash portion, which is designed to provide you with savings on the premiums you put in.

The problem is that the management of these policies comes with high management fees, and low rates of return. The policy we held yielded an annual return of less than 0.5%. Surely, we could have invested that money ourselves in a government bond and done better! The other problem relates to what happens to that cash if you die. The cash portion of your policy is gone. Instead, you are paid the face value of the life insurance portion, which is significantly lower than what you could have purchased for the same amount of money.

We were paying $35 a month for the cash value policy we had. It came with $15,000 worth of life insurance, and over twelve years only yielded a return of the cash we had put in. Shortly before we realized this, we had purchased a term life insurance policy for 25 years, were paying $28 a month, and had coverage of $500,000.

For the same amount of money, we were able to get 33 times the amount of insurance. If we had purchased a term policy for $15,000, we would have paid less than $5 per month, and could have invested the other $30 on our own. That money would have tripled in the same period.

Trust me when I say, you don't want to hold investments in your life insurance policies. The only one who wins is the insurance company.

**Universal Life**—the problem with universal life insurance is that you are paying a significant premium to lock in your rates without having to do a medical later in life. Like we said before, by the time you might need a new policy, your kids should already be out of the house, and your retirement savings should be more than enough to fund your spouse's cost of living. You are self-insured. Not only do you pay 20 times the amount you would for term insurance, the premiums keep increasing the older you get.

Take those excess premiums and invest it yourself.

## STEP 2—DEBT SNOWBALL

Dave Ramsey advises people to pay off our debts using the debt snowball. Essentially, you list your debts from smallest balance to largest balance. Then start paying off your debts one by one. Once you pay the first off, you take the payment amount you were applying to it, and add it onto the next debt's payment. This creates the snowball effect. As you pay off each debt, the payment amounts keep escalating, and the bigger debts will disappear faster than you could have imagined.

It works. In addition, you don't have to worry about interest rates, because the time period in which you are paying off these debts is short enough not to matter. Paying off the first debt will give you the motivation to keep going, and once you see the snowball effect start working, you will understand why it doesn't make sense to consolidate loans. Getting a better interest rate, and lowering your payments don't matter when you are attacking your debt with a vengeance anyways.

Next, we sat down to look at our debts and we worked together on our plan to attack them. We listed our debts from smallest balance to the largest, and made minimum payments on all of them except the smallest. We setup a recurring payment from our chequing account to the smallest loan, so that the money would go to that debt as soon as it came in. Once that line

## CHAPTER 12 - THE IMPROVEMENT PATH

of credit was paid off, we went onto the next. Within 12 months, we paid of over 75% of our debt.

We still had more debt, but made a decision based on what was best for our family. We decided to stop putting excess payments in, and I left my job. My contract was up, and instead of renewing at an amount well below what I needed to make in order to be miserable, I took advantage of my exit clause.

I spent nine months with my kids making up for lost time, before taking a job where I made 50% of what I did before. Why? Because we had rid ourselves of so much debt and cut down on so much of our living expenses (without changing our lifestyle), that we could afford to. We could afford to take a job making less, so that I would have quality time with my family. Time that I will never get back. That was our choice, and it was an amazing choice that has changed my life.

We are now applying the debt snowball, but in a slightly modified fashion. Once our smallest balance car loan is paid off (in just over a year), we will take that monthly payment amount and put it into the other car loan. Just four months after the first is paid off, we will also have paid off the second.

### STEP 3—BUILD A RAINY DAY FUND

Having a rainy day fund in place when I left my job helped me take the time I so desperately needed with my family. The idea behind having three months' worth of your income in savings is to protect yourself from life's bigger surprises. It could be a medical emergency, the loss of your job, or the purchase of your next car. If you have this money set aside, you won't ever have to go into debt again. No matter what.

We continue to use any excess cash flow we have, to save up three months' salary in our emergency fund once again. In fact, we are constantly putting money into our rainy day account. We have a tax-free savings account we make deposits into when we have positive cash flow, and that money is there for emergencies, or other significant family expenses. We use it for other opportunities that present themselves to us from time to time, after talking about what matters in our life. Our rainy day fund allows us to live our life, without having to go out and borrow, or work harder to fund it. It has allowed us so far to meet our goal of not going into any new forms of debt!

We don't save by taking money off our pay, we save by spending less in a month than what we planned, and putting the excess away. You should aim to have 5% of your annual income set aside for a rainy day, after one year of saving. From there, you can continue to add to this account (or invest elsewhere), however you should stop once you get to 50%.

One of the questions I am often asked, is, can I use money in a registered account as my emergency fund?

- ▶ I don't recommend that you have your rainy day funds tied up in a registered account because they aren't as easy to access when Mother Nature calls. Sometimes a rainy day comes when it was totally unexpected. Now you have to sell off investments within the account, let them settle, and then withdraw the funds.

- ▶ I also don't recommend that you have the funds tied up in a registered account because of the tax implications. You will likely pay a withholding tax, and you will need to claim it on your annual return. That $1,000 just dropped by 30% when you took it out. In reality, your emergency fund in this format needs to be 30% higher than one in a regular savings account.

In the end, it is your life. You put it where it makes the most sense for you. We hold some funds in our savings accounts for true emergencies. But we don't hold funds in there for the potential loss of income. That is what our retirement savings are for. We put money in there to lower our tax bill today, and hold it there so we can invest it tax free. And if we do lose our source of income, we are not in a lower tax-bracket, and can afford to withdraw the funds. Is it risky? A little. But I would rather benefit from the tax savings and higher returns, than be so risk averse as to hold it in savings. If I need a job, I can get one. Moreover, if I can't, there are lots of odd jobs to help pay the bills.

## STEP 4—INVEST IN YOURSELF, INCREASE YOUR INCOME

At this point, you have put your values in place; you are living with discipline, and slowly making steps to improve your finances. You have cut down your consumption, and your costs are in line with your life. However, maybe there is still no room for comfort in your budget. You want to pay down your debt faster, and take more vacations with the kids so you can enjoy their youth. I can relate.

You have addressed the root cause of your anxiety with money, but you still feel stuck in the now. You know the way to build a quality life and step up your game is by getting rid of your debt and freeing up your life. However, you aren't sure how the next year will be different than the last.

You are a good parent, and you are doing good things. You

have control over your finances, you value your time more than your money, and you are ready to explore earnings as another source of freedom in your life. Why? Because you will now seek out ways to increase income, without interfering with your ability to be present for your kids, in body, mind, and in spirit. You are going to find something that fits within your long-term plan.

Do I plan to make 50% of what I did before, for the rest of my life? Probably not. I am not quite debt-free, nor do I have enough wealth to retire early. I am not in a position where I am free from the anxiety of money, and like you, I still feel like my money is holding us back a bit. Our mortgage in particular.

We are open to the idea of new or higher sources of income, because we know what money can now provide. Money as a source of freedom aligns with our values. Incremental income that moves us towards our goals faster. Incremental income that doesn't jeopardize the quality of our life as a family.

To start, you have to think about your work from a new perspective. When your kids ask you if you have to work today, you need to be able to answer without frustration in your voice, or in your body. You need to feel like you are going to work, because it is the right thing to do. Because you have made a conscious decision that this job is what is best for you, and is best for your family. You need to go, because it matches your purpose. If it doesn't, you need to start thinking about what you want to do that is different, so that you can feel good about leaving for the office, and model the right things to your kids.

If you could do anything, what would you do? I am talking about living the life of your dreams, while making enough money to fund your life. Write down your goal, and start convincing yourself that you can do it. Start surrounding yourself with people that believe in your newfound purpose, and start learning from them. Start investing in yourself, so that you can invest in your dreams. Create a plan to get you there, and execute.

> I'd rather attempt to do something great and fail, than to attempt to do nothing and succeed.
>
> Robert H. Schuller

In the short term, you may feel trapped in your job or have a job you hate. Nevertheless, as you start to lower your reliance on debt and improve your financial landscape, you will start to see the opportunities you have before you. You will see that if you want more, you need to go get more.

How can I add $500 a month to my income? What talent do I have that can help people? How could I convince people that I can help them?

The answer is simple. Start helping. Your experiences in life are valuable. You may not realize that the struggles you have overcome are similar to what someone else is experiencing in their life right now. The more people you help, the more people will want your help. Moreover, the more people you help, the more people will want to help you. Yes, selflessness still breeds selflessness, and when people start coming to you for things, you are likely to see the abundance that lays before you.

I am amazed now at how much people make per hour, just by doing odd jobs for people. Ask yourself, how can I add easy income to my life? How can I provide value? Maybe it is helping an elderly person in your neighborhood by cleaning their house? Or perhaps it is cutting your sisters grass? Maybe, it's helping someone with their website for their new business?

Whatever it is, you will be surprised at the traction you can gain by helping others, and how one opportunity can lead into another. Eventually, you will figure out what your passion is.

For many of us, we are concerned about how our family and friends might perceive us if they discover we are doing odd jobs. If you are taking odd jobs to help people, trust me when I say, no one cares. Show your kids that helping others, and giving back, is the right thing to do. Show them that it brings you joy and happiness. Show them that it can help you create distance between your income, and your life. Show them that money is about more than trading time: it is about helping people.

How do you get started? Turn off the TV at night. Start reading about ways to improve your life. Stop listening to the radio in the car and download podcasts. Find out how other people are living life on their own terms, and get ideas about how you can too. You will have knowledge today that you didn't yesterday, and you can apply it tomorrow. That is how we make our lives better. One step at a time.

Many people tend to judge people with wealth and assume they either inherited it or came into something quickly. However, what you will discover, is that the journey often takes years. It is a road of self-discovery, which is based on a lot of hard work, and a dedication and passion for helping others. We don't see the hours, days, months, and years that went into developing a life of better. We see them only when they have reached a level of wealth that others aspire to.

## CHAPTER 12 - THE IMPROVEMENT PATH

If you want to up your income, up your game. Improve the people you surround yourself with, and let them show you how to take the journey to financial freedom. Whether your goal is a promotion at work, a new job, or starting out on your own, you need to map out that plan, and work towards it with some intention. Show your kids that living the life you want is possible, when you actively pursue what your passions are.

I believe that you can become clearer on the path you need to take, once you have defined your financial values. When you are on the same page, and in control of your personal finances, your financial health will improve. You will be ready, to embrace an increase in your income, without it increasing your consumption.

## STEP 5—RE-INSTATE YOUR COMPANY MATCH

Every situation is unique, and you need to evaluate these steps in relation to your life. In our situation, we had already been making regular deposits into these retirement and education accounts. Before we started to take some of our positive cash flow and attack the rest of our debt, we asked ourselves a few key questions. Does it make sense to put our contributions on hold for our retirement savings accounts, when I was getting a match from my employer?

I only had to put in 5% of my annual income in order to save 13% toward retirement, and if I opted out, I couldn't opt back in. We made the decision to continue. We also decided to continue with the education savings program, as it was only $50 a month per child.

In a different job, with a different program, I would have likely made a different decision. If there was no match program,

I would have discontinued my retirement savings and put that money directly into our debt snowball. Then, when I got back to this step, I would re-initiate. The short period of time that you take to pay off your debt will pay huge benefits to the cost of your life. You will be a huge step closer to living on your own terms.

## STEP 6—SET YOUR KIDS UP FOR EDUCATION AND LEARNING

We made a similar decision as it relates to our education savings. Where we live, the government matches 20% of our monthly contributions up to a maximum amount. We had opened up these accounts so that any money gifts for the girls could be saved for their future. We also decided (when our income was higher) that we would put $50 per child, per month, into this account.

Should we stop contributing to our kids tax sheltered education plans that are being matched substantially each year by the government? For us, the answer was no.

Some experts recommend having all your debt (with the exception of your house) paid off, and 15% of your income going into retirement, before starting to save for education. I think it depends on the discipline you have, and the choices you and your spouse want to make.

If you stopped at this point however, it is time to start the savings back up again. We are doing this, but our goals are not centered around grades or college. Our savings are centered on providing our kids the opportunity to learn. Whatever route they decide, we will support them, and we are going to encourage a year of experiential learning before they ever go to a traditional post-secondary school. That learning, will prepare them for everything, not just a chosen area of work.

# CHAPTER 13

# GROWTH AND ACCUMULATION

Congratulations again for stepping up your life. You are living your life on your terms, and you are free from the pressure of banks and Facebook newsfeeds. You are ready to pursue what you want, when you want it.

Hopefully, you are already talking about how you can allocate your money so that you will be able to separate your income from your time. Hopefully, you are already taking the time to focus on your relationships and making time spent with your family your number one priority. If you haven't you are ready to!

We have a plan to be debt free, and know the numbers that will get us there. We have figured out we will be 100% debt free in seven years, without having to live a life of sacrifice. On this pace, we would also be able to retire (or exit the time trade) in just 9 years.

We are continuously finding positive cash flow to put into our rainy day fund, we are paying down our debt 100% to plan, we are investing 15% of our income in retirement, we are funding our kids' learning, we have a will and life insurance, and we are managing our money based on our life, not our income.

We are not only accumulating wealth financially I can tell you that we are growing exponentially as people as well. We are modelling more for ourselves, and for our kids. We have realized that growth and accumulation are achievable regardless of how much we have in our bank account.

Once you have reached level three it is time to start planning for your family's future, and use the money that you were using to pay down debt, as an accelerator for other things.

There are three main classes of wealth creation that allow us to move closer to financial freedom, and improve our ability to deepen relationships. Those three classes are:

1. Personal property (real estate)
2. Stocks and bonds (or investing)
3. Business or employment income

Regardless of the method of wealth creation you focus on your purpose should be driven by your ability to continue to free up more of your time to spend on yourself, and your family. Wealth and accumulation should help you create more quality time, with quality people.

## PERSONAL PROPERTY

With interest rates at their lowest of all times, there are several arguments for how you handle personal property. Similar to investing in stocks or bonds, investing in real estate brings risk. Your best way to manage that risk is to accelerate the process of paying off your mortgage. Moreover, once you build enough equity in one, you may want to consider building equity in others.

## CHAPTER 13 - GROWTH AND ACCUMULATION

Each time, focus on accelerating your debt payment schedule, to keep risk as low as possible.

*Paying off your house*—Once you realize how much money you are spending per year on your mortgage, you can start to see how it is affecting all other areas of your life. I remember listening to a podcast on the *Good Dad Project*, about a home equity line of credit. The guest was Jordan Goodman and he talked about using your line of credit to accelerate the payments on your house. In effect, he was advocating a method whereby you could use your positive cash flow to lower your overall cost of borrowing. He indicated you could pay off your house in five years.

Like the accountant I am, I went to work. Three new spreadsheets and a ton of what if scenarios. At first, what I heard him say was "there is a way to get your mortgage paid off without having to create more cash flow." I later realized, that what he meant was "the way to get your mortgage paid off fast, is by creating more cash flow." The idea isn't new at all. It is disguised in a financial advisor's plot to get you to sign up for something you don't necessarily need.

Is there an advantage to the HELOC (Home Equity Line of Credit) program to pay off your mortgage? There is. However, there is such a small amount of interest savings that the risks likely far outweigh the benefits. Again, it is your life, so I'll leave the decision up to you.

I am excited that you are at the point in your life where you want to pay off your house. That is amazing. And the secret for paying off your mortgage faster is...............drum roll please.

Increase your positive cash flow, and pay it off faster.

Sorry if I disappointed you. I know I was disappointed at first too. The truth is, the quicker you pay it off, the less interest you pay. Mortgages are front-end loaded for interest, and for most of us, unavoidable. This my friends is not rocket science. If you use a line of credit to pay off your mortgage, you are making the decision to stand on a trapdoor set by the bank. Shift your weight just a little bit, and you will go crashing through.

I went back to my spreadsheets and pumped out one analysis after another. I analyzed our mortgage and I analyzed our retirement fund. It once again became clear. Even though it is debt on a house, and some would call that good debt, it is still debt. It was holding me back from something more. Something bigger. Something better.

We can provide the kids with everything they need because we figure it out together. We are committed to live that same life going forward. I estimate that we will be 100% debt-free in less than seven years, and we will already have significant amount saved for retirement and our kids' learning.

You can too. Think about what you could do with the money that you free up after you eliminate your mortgage payments. You could work less, and spend more time with your family. Alternatively, you could invest in yourself and your own business, so that you work on your own terms. Perhaps you just want to start spending it on all the things that you want to do in your life, while other people continue to work and struggle between paychecks, you can be living a life of fulfillment. The choice is yours.

It's your life, and your income. How you decide to live it can change your legacy.

Take the payments you were making as part of the debt snowball, and continue to make them on your house. Before you know it, you will be 100% debt free and able to pay for all the things life will throw at you. You will invest and growth wealth, faster than you could have ever imagined, and your money will begin to work harder than you can.

I still today, remember when my parents paid off their house. They were in their forties. I don't know why, but it is something that stuck with me from my childhood. I know that I will celebrate that moment in our lives more than my parents even did. It will be an amazing, teachable moment for my kids, and create an opportunity to talk about starting your career by living based on your life, and not your income.

Once you have paid off at least 50% of the value in your home, or you have saved up enough from your investments, you may also consider investing in more property. Rental property. It is something I am working through right now.

Create a five-year plan and set a target of purchasing one home per year. If you plan to use equity from your current home (and you have more than 50% of equity), I would recommend keeping the down payment amount on the second property to less than 15% of your principal home value. This will help protect you against a 20% correction in housing prices. With the purchase of your first home, figure out everything you need to know about property management and create a systematic approach to this new business area in your life. Once you have created the system, move on to your second home. Real estate, done properly, can allow you to increase wealth exponentially.

## STOCKS AND BONDS

Whether it is mutual funds, dividend paying stocks, or ETFs (Exchange Traded Funds), how you use your cash to invest and accumulate wealth is entirely up to you. There are a lot of resources that you can find about investing. My only recommendation is to keep it simple. Diversify enough so that you are not dependant on one stock, but not so much that you eliminate your earning potential. I recommend investing in three or four good mutual funds, in the growth and income categories. Find mutual funds that have a proven track record over the past 10 to 15 years, and have a compounded growth rate of 10% or more.

If you choose to utilize the services of a financial planner, it is important that you find one that is interested in looking at your entire financial situation and giving you the tools and resources to address each. If they are more concerned on products than personal growth, keep looking.

## BUSINESS AND EMPLOYMENT INCOME GROWTH

What are the ways we are looking at increasing income? We have reviewed several. Starting our own business, going back to being a two-income household, getting a job that pays more, trading more of our time for money, or investing in things today, that will generate passive income tomorrow.

We will likely do all of these, but we will do it on our terms. We will do it in ways that show our kids what it means to be more. We will do it in a way that ignites passion and drives a higher purpose. We will do it to up our life!

When opportunities present themselves, we owe it to

ourselves as parents to take advantage of them. We owe it to our kids to show them that living the life of our dreams is possible and not reserved for someone else. We must embrace that next challenge, and take our life to the next level.

Take the steps you need to take, and push away the fears that are currently holding you back. Your fears are meant to protect you, but recognize that the source of those fears is based on your past. A past that you are ready to leave behind in hopes for something better. Don't let your past hold you back from creating a better version of yourself. Don't let your fears hold your family back from something more.

## MODEL MORE

Now that we are in a new phase of our life, it is important not to lose sight of the bigger goal here. Your kids. You have significantly changed your family's finances and modelled healthy values for you kids. Your children are comfortable talking about money, and they don't see it as something taboo. They have been involved in family decisions about money, and they haven't felt like they have lived a life of sacrifice. They are well-positioned to be more as well.

Nevertheless, there are still a lot of moments in our lives where we have the opportunity to talk about money on our kids' level. I call them teachable moments. There is also a level of responsibility we hold as parents, related to the education we provide to our kids on personal finance. We need to set them up to handle life's challenges in a way that is healthy for their money, healthy for their relationships, and healthy for themselves. In ways that perhaps we didn't.

# CHAPTER 14

# TEACH IN THE MOMENT

Your kids are the most important thing in your life. I get it. Nevertheless, being the most important doesn't always mean they come first. If you want to create a model of happiness, there are times in your life where you need to invest in yourself and your marriage before all else. You need to invest the time in controlling your finances, if you want to be able to teach your kids. Create your values, figure out what level you are currently at, and then take the steps to change your financial landscape. As soon as you have started, you will see that you are ready to take advantage of the teachable moments that arise in your everyday life.

As my wife often reminds me, 80% of what you teach to your kids about daily finances should be through your actions. Only 20% should come through your words.

Our financial teaching needs to develop as our kids develop. Our goal is to instil the values we talked about earlier through a combination of actions and words. Here are some quick strategies which will help you do that.

## CHAPTER 14 - TEACH IN THE MOMENT

## THE TODDLER YEARS

Once your child is ready for pre-school, they have likely started to learn that there are different types of consequences, to each of their actions. When it comes to our kids' safety or well-being, we do place expectations on them. Certain things in our kids' lives are just not negotiable, because there could be catastrophic results from their actions if we don't place those expectations on them.

In our house, we also put certain household expectations in here too, like cleaning up after themselves. You need to figure out what works best in your house.

All other items that are not safety related, we try to let them learn based on consequences. Moreover, when possible, we try to avoid negative consequences and focus on either natural consequences, or value based consequences, for our learning moments.

Natural based consequences happen by letting kids learn through the result of their own actions. For example, if they choose to lean back on their chair, we don't yell at them to stop. We provide them with the information they need to make their own decision, and then they need to live with the consequences that result from their choices. If they choose to ignore the information we presented, chances are the natural consequence will help them learn in time anyways. They only have to fall off the chair once or twice to learn that lesson.

Value based consequences give us the opportunity for money moments. Using a money reward system, we can encourage our kids with a few opportunities to help others and add value. When they do, there is a financial reward for it. We believe that kids need to learn to take care of themselves, and their things, but when they help other people they are providing a value that may be rewarded. We pay them as soon as we see the behavior, so that they are able to associate the value to the reward. You will be surprised at how well toddlers take to this type of learning. Just don't go overboard, and limit it to one or two things.

## THE CHILDHOOD YEARS

Now that your kids are growing, the list of things they want is likely growing as well. This is a time to teach them that Mom and Dad will not be funding every little thing in their life. They need to take on some additional chores if they want to buy additional things. Buy them the necessities, and let them save up for their wants.

While you increase the chores they can be paid for you also need to increase your household expectations. We must do some things because they are part of living. Making their bed, cleaning up their own dishes, putting their clothes away, and taking the trash out, are all examples of household expectations. Make the chores something bigger than normal household expectations, and provide a different level of reward based on the complexity of the task.

## THE TEENAGE YEARS

There are several different types of teachable moments you can create with your kids once they are old enough to generally look after themselves. You should now be focusing on values and taking more opportunities to talk about money. Remember that they will not learn about finances in school, and you only have

CHAPTER 14 - TEACH IN THE MOMENT

a few years to teach them on a daily basis. Live your values, and sit down with your kids to create a saving, spending, investing, and giving plan. Set some goals for them as it relates to the portion of their education they need to fund, and then let them loose to learn from their own mistakes. Whether they are doing significant chores around the house, are doing odd jobs around the neighborhood, taking freelance jobs online, or working at a part-time job, they should be saving up for their life.

But Jeff, how can I make sure they don't blow all their money? By living the values you've created for them. They should have a budget, and you should be reviewing it with them once per month. Each meeting presents yet another opportunity to teach them about money.

Throughout each of these phases in your kids' lives, you need to communicate with them. Involve them in decisions the family makes, and let them make some mistakes. They need to know that failure is an option, and through failure we grow. Create a safe place for your kids to learn valuable lessons about finances and about life, and you will create a future that is based on more.

## FINANCIAL INTELLIGENCE

Now that you are teaching in the moment, we need to address the bigger issue of financial education. Our school systems today will not teach your kids how money works, what it can and cannot provide you, and how to create wealth. You need to find a way to teach these things to your kids more formally than modelling a different set of behaviours. Use this book, and find others as well, then create a plan to teach your kids the specifics. Once they are old enough to participate, involve them in all of your budgeting meetings, task them with reviewing your investments, and get on the same page with your family's financial plans.

Schools also won't teach your kids about financial statements, return on investment, or how to read a cash flow statement. Moreover, they don't talk about risk management, entrepreneurship, or taxes. If you want your kids to learn these essential life skills, you need to learn them too. Find them the books that they need to read, and together create a set of exercises to allow them to learn the skills required. And just maybe, if you are humble enough, you will share the experience and learn them together from someone else!

# CHAPTER 15

# BALANCING WORK, LIFE, & FAMILY

How you balance work, life, and family is going to be different from how your neighbour does. What is important is that you figure out the best way to balance it for you, and do it in a way that is best for the legacy you want to leave.

As a parent, you have a lot of stuff on the go. Not only do you have to make enough money to feed your family and pay for your house, you have to manage new clothes for every season, extra-curricular activities, birthday party gifts, and all the other things that your kids surprise you with each week. You are working hard and running around so much you barely know if you are coming or going. I get it.

The first and most important step in finding balance in your life is to start living in the moment.

If you want to find true happiness, look within. Focus on what is important in life, and be in the moment enough to appreciate it. Being in the moment feels good. Being in the moment allows you to find joy and passion in the times when you are doing things you don't like. It is that small moment or subtle connection that makes those things seem worthwhile. It is those moments that you will feel in your heart, and it is those moments that you will learn to love.

For me, it is important to live a good life, and to learn and to grow. It is important to connect to people, and it is important to help. When I do these things, I feel happy.

I can't always spend the time I want to at work, but when I am there I can make it quality time. I can't always spend the time I want to at home with my family, but when I am there, I can make it better time.

**I can be in the moment.**

**I can listen. I can listen to learn. And if I must, I can listen to communicate.**

I am more grateful today than I have ever been. And I am in the moment more and more every day! Now that I have begun to align everything in my life towards a clear purpose, it is easy to see which decisions are best for me, and which are best for my family. Income was not our problem, consumption was.

As long as we had addressed the consumption problem, income could start to help. In fact, when we started down this new path with our finances, generating income was the very first thing we did. We purged (instead of splurging), and quickly brought in the necessary money to get us into a cash positive position. The sale of our material things turned our budget around, and then also started to provide us with the emergency funds we so desperately needed.

After we found a quick source of income, we set out on our journey to create stability. Stability through our working budget. We began spending based on our budget, and instilled a newfound discipline in our lives. We paid down debt, and put ourselves in a position of significantly less stress. We needed to do these things in order to create a better future for our family. And we did.

Now, we are open to the idea of increasing income, so we can accelerate our plan. So, we can embrace freedom and do the things we want, on our terms. So, we can live the life dreams are made of.

I have written about my story and how I struggled to find balance. How I found the courage to quit the job I had worked so hard to get, knowing that it was going to mean financial sacrifice. I did it because it was better for us on all levels. In addition, I think it is important to share another perspective as well. Gene is an amazing person I have connected with over the past year, and he inspires me every day. Here is his story!

## GENE VILLENEUVE

*When I look back at the last 25 years of my career and my financial success, I realize I have a unique relationship with money. I always saw it as a means and not the ends. I made experiences, growth, family, relationships, and continuous learning the top priority. Along the way, money covered my basic costs. I was too busy building my career, my family, and a portfolio of experiences to bother focusing on money. As long as my hair looked presentable, I was fit, ate well, and dressed professionally I was spending enough.*

*I think my first real career out of university launched me into a different perspective on money and jobs. I was thrust into a career of travel where most of my expenses were paid and I was able to* see the world. These formative years etched an unending desire to jump at new opportunities and experiences, and to travel the world. I didn't have to spend a lot of my own money, yet I was still able to explore the world and meet people from new cultures. I still remember walking the streets of Damascus as a 24-year-old, making friends with Syrians based on sign language, drinking tea, smiling, and laughing.

Some people live a frugal life, make safe choices, and stay tied to their job because they feel it is their only path to financial wealth. If they want any chance of breaking free of the life sentence they are in, they must continue to save manically and frugally. I was taught to live frugally because in my family money was tight. I grew up in a family that focused on savings, because that the only way we saw out. When I began my career, I made a conscious decision not to put myself into a financial noose with a mortgage and a fancy car loan. Instead, I paid off my student loans within a year of graduation and didn't own a car until I was 29. The first car I bought was a used Honda Civic for $4500. I also continued living in student apartments until my early 30s. I took a different perspective to improving our finances. I now looked at both savings, and income.

If I could find interesting and challenging jobs, be willing to relocate and take the risks, I could increase my earnings as a by-product of the roles I took on. As long as I didn't spend all my income on silly things I would always have the cash and the portfolio to fall back on.

And this is exactly what happened. Successively my spending power increased. I remember when I bought my first new car. I went into the dealer and paid cash for it. I recall thinking to

## CHAPTER 15 - BALANCING WORK, LIFE, & FAMILY

myself... I could buy this car 20 times and still not go into debt. Having that kind of money gave me the confidence to take more career risks. I knew that if things didn't work out I would be ok.

Eventually I got married and with a child on the way we moved back to Canada to establish roots and we bought a house. As we had saved significant amounts of cash, we bought a house and paid nearly 80% on the value. That wasn't all of our money. We kept an emergency reserve and didn't touch our retirement funds. This way, our mortgage would be low and we would continue saving large percentages of my income every month.

Today my wife and I are debt free and could retire by most Canadian standards. But I'm not wired that way. I enjoy learning, going out on the limb, and seeing what my limits are. I live the life I want, regardless of how much I make. Now that I have children in primary school, I have slowed down my career changes so that I can provide consistency in their lives. I am there for their events like ballet, swimming, running, and horseback riding. I am there to play with them in the evenings and on weekends if I wish. I moved to Europe so that I could eliminate being on the road for long periods, and in the process created a new life experience for my kids.

I managed risk by being frugal, but we grew our wealth by making career decisions based on the good of our family. By building a vast and respected business network, taking risks, and learning from both my successes and failures, I was able to build my career and increase my earnings. To this day, we still spend wisely, but we add more experiences into our lives every day. We treasure our weekend trips around Paris, our ski holidays in the Alps, or our vacations in Provence and Italy. We do these by getting *reasonable accommodations, renting the least expensive cars and taking inexpensive transportation. We spend money on good food, and make spending time together more important, than spending money on each other.*

*Today our money is working for us. Our house in Canada is rented and provides reasonable positive cash flow that goes back into the house in improvements, or it goes into our savings. Our portfolio is invested mostly in dividend stocks, where the dividends fund our RESPs, and TFSAs each year. Anything extra goes right back into buying more stock. Over time, the objective is to retire on a dividend stream. When will we? It doesn't matter right now, as we are happy living the lifestyle we want, regardless of the income we earn.*

*Throughout my career and still to this day, I make family time and personal time a priority. I run three to four days a week, eat healthy diet, and am proud of the bond I have with my family.*

Amazing and inspiring story! What you see from Gene's life, and my story, is that they both centre on one thing. Living for a bigger purpose. Living for the love of your family. Living in the moment, being grateful for what we have, and creating real human connections. That is how you will find balance. That is how we find happiness.

Spending nine months home with your family when they are young has the power to change your perspective on life. I no longer want to trade away my time to help others become rich, and miss the important things in my kids' lives. I no longer see money as the tool to buy things: I see it as the vehicle that provides freedom. The freedom to do what I want with my family, when I want to do it. Heck, when I need to do it.

## CHAPTER 15 - BALANCING WORK, LIFE, & FAMILY

As a parent, you want the best for your kids and the best for your family. The best is a relative term, and is defined differently depending on whom you talk to. I want to show my kids how to be more. How to live life on their terms, and take happiness from the relationships in their life. I want to show my kids that they have the power to replace the life society tells them to live, and live the life they are destined for. I want to show them that we are all unique, and that we can create our own success story. I want them to see me, model a life of possibility, based on embracing your fears and taking risks. I want them to help others, without worrying about what others think of them.

To do that I needed to see money for what it was: a source of freedom instead of a source of things. I needed to embrace my failures as a son, father, husband, and as a leader. I needed my children to know that admitting your failures, does not make you weak, it makes you human. And I am human.

I want my kids to embrace the failures they make with money over the course of their life, and learn from them. I want them to try to be better every day, and understand the true value that money affords us. Freedom. The freedom to build relationships and forge bonds. The freedom to be happy in life's moments. The freedom to be.

# WRAP UP

Your personal finances are about choice. You can earn more, or spend less. Ideally, you will choose what's right for you and your family, when you need to.

I freed myself from trading time for money, and started living my life. I found a new way. I see my kids every morning and have the time to enjoy breakfast with them when I choose to. I have the freedom to come and go as I please, because I am unshackled from my work. When I am with my kids, I am not thinking about work, and I am home for dinner every day now.

We have started using our budget to manage our expenses, and we are cutting out the things that we don't need in our life. I have cut out pop and reduced the sugar I put in my coffee. We stopped buying packaged food if we could make the things ourselves. We order less food when we go out to eat, and at times, we are making the decision to drive instead of having drinks when we are out, so that we don't have to spend money on cabs. By making healthier financial choices, we are living healthier lives.

We used to spend freely on vacations and get rooms with bedrooms for everyone. We bought all of our meals at restaurants, and rushed around taking in everything we could. It was stressful and expensive, and in the end, didn't make for an enjoyable vacation for us as parents. We have changed all that, and today get rooms that we can afford, buy groceries and have fresh fruit in our room, and make decisions together on what activities we are going to partake in. We spend 50% less than what we did before, are less stressed, and have become closer as a family. It turns out being close brings you closer.

Will implementing the steps in this book make you a millionaire? Not by themselves. However, they do have power to enrich your lives in ways you never dreamed of. They can help you strengthen your relationship with your spouse, and they can help you free your mind, so that you can be more present for your kids in every way.

Do these steps apply to you? I believe they apply to everyone. Even though this book is about parents, it applies to anyone who wishes to embrace them.

Let me provide an example on how these steps could apply. I talked to someone recently who explained they had no debt other than their mortgage, they had enough saved up for a rainy day, and they had started to invest in their retirement. They were a young couple that were about to get married, and had been living in a house together for some time. They were trying to decide whether to put in a pool or have a very large wedding.

I asked them if they had money saved up for either, or did they have to borrow money to have them? They were going to borrow. I then asked if they had ever thought of paying off their mortgage.

They didn't see it as a priority, because they were doing so well with money.

"If you did pay down your mortgage, and you weren't happy without it, couldn't you just get another one?" I asked.

I then asked if they could save up the cash to pay for either the pool or the wedding, so that they could enjoy it without the burden of the payments. They said they didn't want to wait three years to do either.

In my own mind, I immediately started to question their level of financial health. How successfully were they in managing their money if it was going to take three years to save up enough money to put a pool in? Did they have financial values? Were they making decisions together, based on a working budget?

Like so many others, the tendency in this day and age when we get ourselves out of debt is to want to go right back in. Instead of taking the excess cash flow and investing it for retirement, saving it for our kids' learning, for paying down our mortgage, or for growing and accumulating wealth, we go out and use that cash flow to get another loan to pay off. I did this most of my life.

Today, my wife and I save up to buy the things we want in life. We realize that if we want something bad enough, we should be able to save up to buy it. We control our money, so that it doesn't end up controlling us!

I love that this couple wants to live their life now, and I love that they were talking about money! I just question whether a big wedding or a pool will bring them the happiness they are looking for, when they don't have the money to do either. I trust and hope they figure out what is best for them.

You could be living debt-free but spending all of your excess cash flow living the life you want right now. But what lessons would you be teaching your kids? How much time are you spending working, and being away from your family, in order to be able to spend so freely? Do you and your spouse talk openly about finances in front of your kids? Do you talk openly with our kids?

My wife and I communicate better than we ever have, and we are laughing more than we ever did before. Our kids are getting the thing they wanted most from us: time. We are living off less, but are present so much more. By controlling our finances, we have taken back control of our lives. We have created a new normal.

## LET'S CREATE SOMETHING MORE

If we can make this change, you can too. I was not inspired by my own story for two decades. I didn't know that it was even worth telling. But I have realized that we all have a story, and it is worth admitting it, embracing it, and sharing it with others. I took the time, and was fortunate to change the way I approached my life. I have taken steps forward instead of back, by putting one foot in front of the other and moving ahead with intention. I am focused on how my actions and my words, impact others.

I have learned that wealth and happiness doesn't come from the number of things you own, but rather from the people you have in your life, and the time you get to spend with them. I want my kids to have the opportunity to be more. I want to show them that we can live the life we want, and that we all have the opportunity to be more.

I now have a higher purpose. I want our kids to get the financial education they need to better handle the challenges they will face in their life. I want our kids to love themselves and develop themselves, so they can deepen the relationships they have in their life. And for them to do that, we as parents need to take an active role in educating our kids on these three areas of their life.

We need to teach our kids how to handle money, how to build relationship skills, and how to develop their health and well-being. We need to do it, because our school system won't.

Create a higher purpose as a parent so that your kids are better equipped to handle the darkest times in their lives, in ways we simply couldn't.

The steps outlined in this book will help you make incremental improvements to your financial health, without regard for the money you have in your bank account. These steps will help you model behaviours that will show your kids how to be more, instead of wanting more. These steps can work for you. They can work for anyone.

It is never too late to improve your finances, or your life. Start today and shape a different future for the parents of today, and for the parents of tomorrow.

CPSIA information can be obtained
at www.ICGtesting.com
Printed in the USA
LVOW10s1225100117
520406LV00001B/2/P